THE BOOK OF ISAIAH

IN FIFTEEN STUDIES

REVISED EDITION

GEORGE L. ROBINSON

Professor of Biblical Literature and English Bible,
Presbyterian Theological Seminary
Chicago, Illinois

BAKER BOOK HOUSE
GRAND RAPIDS 6, MICHIGAN
1954

PHOTOLITHOPRINTED BY CUSHING - MALLOY, INC.
ANN ARBOR, MICHIGAN, UNITED STATES OF AMERICA
1954

To
My Students
Past and Present

CONTENTS

CONTENTS

10 CONTENTS

12 CONTENTS

INTRODUCTION

Few books of the Old Testament have in modern times received the attention which has been accorded the book of Isaiah. An unusual flood of critical and expository literature has recently appeared, to which no careful student of the book would deny his very great indebtedness.

Yet it must be confessed that the divisive criticism of Isaiah has developed into a sort of reckless surgery, until it has become well-nigh impossible to find a proof text in support of a reasonably conservative position, whose genuineness is not disputed by someone. It almost seems sometimes that doubt were in competition with doubt. As Whitehouse remarks in opposition to Lagarde, Duhm and Marti, who dissect Isa. 63: 1, " as Edom is thus eliminated in one clause, it is necessary to operate on Bozrah in the other." (New Century Bible, *Isaiah,* vol. II., p. 303, n. 2.) The same is true of hosts of other passages.

Yet notwithstanding the truth of these statements (and who would deny their truthfulness?) it is better to keep an open mind concerning the origin of these prophecies and not foreclose inquiry. For the book of Isaiah is a marvelous piece of literature even when dismembered and treated as an anthology or collection of prophecies from various prophets in different ages. And surely God could have inspired twenty Isaiahs as well as one! The supreme question is, Have we adequate or convincing proof of the book's alleged composite character? In the judgment of the present writer we have not.

The book of Isaiah when treated as an organic whole is a grand masterpiece. One great purpose dominates the author throughout, which, as he proceeds, is brought to a climax in a picture·of Israel's redemption and the glorification of Zion.

Failure to recognize this unity incapacitates a man to do it exegetical justice. Of no other book in the Old Testament are the words of Davidson more true than of Isaiah, that " no particular doctrine of the prophet can be properly understood without some comprehension of his scheme of thought as a whole."

The divine name, " the Holy One of Israel," which Isaiah ascribes to Jehovah, and which occurs twenty-five times in his book and only six times elsewhere in the entire Old Testament, interlocks inseparably all the various portions with one another and stamps them with the personal imprimatur of him who saw the vision of the Majestic God seated upon his throne high and lifted up, and heard the angelic choirs singing, " Holy, holy, holy, is Jehovah of hosts: the whole earth is full of his glory " (chapter 6). The presence of this divine name in all the different portions of the book is of more value in identifying Isaiah as the author of these prophecies than though his name had been inscribed at the beginning of every chapter (cf. 1: 4; 5: 19, 24; 10: 20; 12: 6; 17: 7; 29: 19; 30: 11, 12, 15; 31: 1; 37: 23—that is, twelve times in chapters 1-39; and 41: 14, 16, 20; 43: 3, 14; 45: 11; 47: 4; 48: 17; 49: 7; 54: 5; 55: 5; 60: 9, 14 —or thirteen times in chapters 40-66).

One great theme likewise binds in a peculiar way all parts of this great book together, namely, *salvation by faith*. Isaiah is the Saint Paul of the Old Testament. His book taken as a whole is a large and illustrated Hebrew edition, so to speak, of the Epistle to the Romans; the essential difference between the apostle and the prophet being, that Isaiah lived in the future of Israel's theology, whereas Paul correlated the teachings of the past. *Prediction* is the very essence and core of Isaiah's entire message. His verb tenses are predominatingly futures and prophetic perfects. Isaiah was pre-eminently *a prophet of the Future*. With unparalleled suddenness he repeatedly leaps from despair to hope, from threat to promise, from the actual to the ideal. More than any other prophet also he demonstrates the interrelation of the natural and supernatural, showing that their spheres overlap. Isaiah's theology is the divinest and therefore the profoundest in the Old Testament. His statement that he " saw the Lord " (6: 1) is none too strong to account for the heights to which his imagination soars.

No wonder that, when Augustine shortly after his conversion asked Ambrose which of the sacred books he should begin first to study, the answer he received was, " The prophecies of Isaiah." And considering the statesmanship of the prophet it is likewise little wonder that the celebrated British orator, Edmund Burke, habitually read from the prophecies of Isaiah before going to Parliament. The book of Isaiah is a marvelously profound, unique and exhaustive monograph on the doctrine of temporal and spiritual salvation. And the most marvelous thing about it is the fact that such truths were actually apprehended and committed to writing by anyone *before* the time of Christ; for the book of Isaiah is "the gospel before the Gospel."

Most humbly, therefore, the author sends forth this brief exposition of Isaiah's great book in the hope that it may at least *prepare the way* for a saner and deeper exposition of the great eighth century prophet, and at the same time bring relief to those whose minds are so often distracted by the technical and frequently misleading critical commentaries upon it. Perhaps no book of the Old Testament has suffered more from commentary interference than that of Isaiah.

For many helpful suggestions the author is indebted to his friend, the Reverend Lewis Gaston Leary, Ph. D., of New York, who not only reviewed the ms. in advance, but has kindly assisted in reading the proof sheets and in preparing the index.

The American Standard Revision is the Bible text used in quotation. The student should be careful to read the Prophet himself, chapter by chapter and section by section as indicated in the Studies, before consulting the exposition.

Preface to the 1938 Edition

A full quarter of a century has passed since the first appearance of this little handbook on Isaiah. Frequently through the years my friends have asked me, " Do you still believe in the unity of Isaiah?" and frankly I have invariably answered: " Am more convinced than ever."

But, to champion the unity of the book is by no means my prime purpose in republishing. The great majority of people in the pew, or even of students of theology, care little whether there are two Isaiahs or twenty. Those who do care usually assume that the book must be divided, and leave it there.

My only claim is that no modern critical theory of disintegration has solved the problem, or proven satisfactory to scholars. Recent theories are as indecisive and unconvincing as they were twenty-five years ago. Old arguments used to prove disintegration have in many cases been discarded, and those newly proposed, unfortunately to some of us, seem as nonsequential and ephemeral as those abandoned.

What is most needed today is *readers of the book itself*. Indeed, what the pulpit needs most of all today is, in our judgment, men who are thoroughly equipped *to teach the Bible*. The pulpit has lost interest to many because too many have lost their Bible. The chief reason, therefore, for republishing these " Studies " is to help make the Book of Isaiah more intelligible to those who are willing to study.

George L. Robinson.

Chicago, Illinois, November, 1938

THE DEAD SEA SCROLL

Let me preface this new edition of this handbook on Isaiah with a few remarks concerning the Dead Sea Scroll.

The discovery in 1947 of the complete text in Hebrew of the book of Isaiah in a Cave near the north end of the Dead Sea, about seven miles south of Jericho, is of special interest and of paramount importance to all thoughtful Bible students. The manuscript is dated, by most archaeological specialists, as having been written probably during the first century B.C. (possibly a little before), which is well nigh one thousand years earlier than the oldest Hebrew manuscripts of the Massoretes became known.

The text of the newly discovered Scroll, having been carefully examined by scholars, is found to correspond almost perfectly with the contents of our present Bibles, both Hebrew and English: "without either additions, omissions, or alterations of any major importance." Even scribal errors have been corrected by the scribe himself. Naturally the Scroll has no vowel-signs, as they were not added to the consonants till supplied by the Massoretes centuries later.

Nor has the Scroll any colophons, or marks to separate one section from another. For example, Chapter 40:1, "Comfort ye, comfort ye" is written close to the last verse of Chapter 39, the scribe actually writing it on the last line of space left on the page. The Scribe thus brings the "comforts" of the Incomparable God in Chap. 40 into closest possible connection with the "threats" of Chap. 39: apparently quite unconscious of the critical idea that they were written centuries apart! The scribe may be teaching us! The unity of the book is not a mere modern opinion.

In general, let me say, that to deny the unity of the Book of Isaiah, as a whole, creates more difficulties than it explains. The very *Title* of the Book tells us that Isaiah had "visions"; i.e., revelations of God, which he was commissioned, as the human amanuensis, to record.

George L. Robinson

Chicago, Illinois. Jan. 22, 1954

And One Cried unto Another, and Said, Holy, Holy, Holy, is Jehovah of Hosts: the Whole Earth is Full of His Glory.

And I Heard the Voice of the Lord, Saying, Whom Shall I Send, and Who Will Go for Us? Then I Said, Here Am I; Send Me.

ISA. 6: 3, 8.

How Beautiful upon the Mountains are the Feet of Him That Bringeth Good Tidings, That Publisheth Peace, That Bringeth Good Tidings of Good, That Publisheth Salvation, That Saith unto Zion, Thy God Reigneth!

ISA. 52: 7.

STUDY ONE

Isaiah's Personal History

1. Of the four great prophets—Amos and Hosea, Isaiah and Micah—who are known to have lived and labored during the last half of the eighth century B. C., Isaiah is the greatest; indeed, Isaiah is the king of all prophets.

2. He bore a name symbolic of his message, namely, Isaiah, signifying "Jehovah saves." He was a citizen, probably a native, of Jerusalem; hence a city prophet. In all his messages he gives great prominence to the capital. Inasmuch also as he stood in closest relations to the king, he was a court preacher.

3. He was the son of Amoz (not Amos). He sprang apparently from a family of some rank, as may be inferred from his easy access to the king (Isa. 7), and his close intimacy with the priest (8: 2). Tradition makes him the cousin of King Uzziah.

4. Isaiah was married and had at least two sons; to whom he gave the names, Shear-jashub, "a remnant shall return" (7: 3), and Maher-shalal-hash-baz, "hasting to the spoil, hurrying to the prey" (8: 2, 3), symbolic of Assyria's mad lust of conquest. These names, as also his own, Isaiah regarded as embodying his message to Judah and Jerusalem (8: 18).

Isaiah's Call to be Prophet

1. Isaiah was called in the year that King Uzziah died. While worshiping in the temple he fell into a trance; suddenly the house and the ministers became transfigured, and he beheld in triple vision God, sin, and salvation. He also received a call and a commission which sent him on a new pathway of duty (Isa. 6).

2. From that moment, he seems to have regarded prophecy as his life's work. He responded with noteworthy alacrity, though he knew from the outset that his task was to be one of fruitless warning and judgment (6: 9-13). Nevertheless, without reserve, he dedicated to the work not only himself but his family. He speaks of his wife as the " prophetess " (8: 3), and of course the names of his two sons were constant reminders of the nation's fate. He also gathered about him a coterie of " disciples " to whom he committed his oracles of hope and promise (8: 16).

3. Having been brought up in Jerusalem, Isaiah doubtless received the best education the capital could supply. He knew not only books but men; consequently he was well fitted to become the political and religious counselor of the nation. He must have known the prophets Amos and Hosea, and often heard at least echoes of their preaching to North Israel. He probably had many a conference with Micah, his younger contemporary in Judah, and frequently heard men tell of the earthquake which occurred in Uzziah's reign (Amos 1: 1; Zech. 14: 5).

4. But the event which impressed him most was the vision of the majestic and thrice holy God which he saw in the temple (6: 3). This left an indelible impression upon his soul, and more than anything else fitted him for his difficult life work. Chapter 6 is technically the only " vision " in his book; and yet no other book of the Old Testament is so completely a continued vision of the future. For Isaiah the death-year of King Uzziah had more than mere chronological value; it was the supreme moment of his spiritual history.

Isaiah's Political and Spiritual Horizon

1. No Hebrew prophet ever lived whose political horizon, domestic and foreign, was wider or more

extended than that of Isaiah of the eighth century
B. C. Syria, Assyria, Babylonia, Egypt, Philistia,
Ammon, Moab and Edom were all actors upon the
ever-changing stage of history.

2. Only God can bound a man's spiritual horizon. He indeed spake " of old time unto the fathers in the prophets by divers portions," but who
would dare premise just how large the " portion "
was which He committed to Isaiah of Jerusalem?
Whether or not Isaiah wrote all the prophecies of
the wonderful book which for so long has been
associated with his name, humanly speaking such
a book might more easily have been composed in
his age than in any other.

3. The theme about which all his prophecies re-
volve is " Judah and Jerusalem " (1: 1). Even in
the oracles addressed to foreign nations (chapters
13-23), Judah and Jerusalem are still the goal and
center of the prophet's thoughts. Occasionally,
however, he directed a brief message to North
Israel, as in chapters 9: 8—10: 4; 17: 1-11; 28:
1-6; and frequently he interspersed his prophecies
with history as occasion required (chapters 7, 20,
and 36-39).

4. His mission to his own age was a very com-
prehensive one; so much so that Delitzsch speaks
of him as " the universal prophet of Israel." There
were practically no bounds to his imagination, any
more than there were limits to Jehovah's power to
save (45: 22). Isaiah saw clearly that the ideal
kingdom, which God was about to establish
through the Messiah, included all people. In a
word, he was the prophet of universal redemption
by faith.

Isaiah's Character and Patriotism

1. No prophet of the Old Testament combined
more perfectly than Isaiah earthly wisdom and sa-
gacity, courage and conviction, versatility of gifts
and singleness of purpose, on the one hand, with

clear vision and spiritual intuition, a love of righteousness and a keen appreciation of Jehovah's majesty and holiness, on the other. Valeton describes him thus: "Never perhaps has there been another prophet like Isaiah, who stood with his head in the clouds and his feet on the solid earth, with his heart in the things of eternity and with mouth and hand in the things of time, with his spirit in the eternal counsel of God and his body in a very definite moment of history."

2. No prophet also, except perhaps Jeremiah, felt more keenly than Isaiah the cost of genuine patriotism, or the burden which all true prophets in every age are forced to bear. He saw clearly that a man cannot be a faithful patriot and always be optimistic, saying complimentary things about his nation or their deeds.

3. Isaiah was no soothsayer. Frequently he denounced heathen cults as inimical to the theocracy. In politics he was neutral; but he did not separate religion from politics. As a seer he united the profoundest religious insight with a wide knowledge of men and affairs, and possessed a balance of powers rarely combined in a single individual. He was unquestionably the most imposing figure of his age.

Isaiah's Literary Genius and Style

1. For versatility of expression and brilliancy of imagery Isaiah had no superior, not even a rival. His style marks the climax of Hebrew literary art. Both his periods and descriptions are most finished and sublime. "Every word from him stirs and strikes its mark," says Dillmann. Beauty and strength are characteristic of his entire book. He is a perfect artist in words. No other Old Testament writer uses so many beautifully picturesque illustrations (5: 1-7; 12: 3; 28: 23-29; 32: 2).

2. Epigrams and metaphors, particularly of

flood, storm and sound (1: 13; 5: 18, 22; 8: 8;
10: 22; 28: 17, 20; 30: 28, 30), interrogation and
dialogue (10: 8; 6: 8), antithesis and alliteration
(1: 18; 3: 24; 17: 10, 12), hyperbole and parable
(2: 7; 5: 1-7; 28: 23-29), even paranomasia, or
play on words (5: 7; 7: 9), characterize Isaiah's
book as the masterpiece of Hebrew literature. He
is also famous for his vocabulary and richness of
synonyms. Ezekiel uses 1535 words; Jeremiah,
1653; the Psalmists, 2170; Isaiah, 2186.

3. Isaiah was also an orator. Jerome likened
him to Demosthenes. He was likewise a poet. He
frequently elaborates his messages in rhythmic or
poetic style (12: 1-6; 25: 1-5; 26: 1-12; 38: 10-
20; 42: 1-4; 49: 1-9; 50: 4-9; 52: 13—53: 12; 60-
62; 66: 5-24); and in several instances slips into
elegiac rhythm: for example, in 37: 22-29 there
is a fine taunting poem on Sennacherib, and in 14:
4-21 another on the king of Babylon. As Driver
remarks, " Isaiah's poetical genius is superb."

Traditions Concerning Isaiah's Martyrdom

1. Nothing historically definite is known concerning the prophet's end. There was a tradition,
however, common among the Jews towards the
close of the second century A. D., to the effect that
Isaiah suffered martyrdom in the heathen reaction
which occurred under King Manasseh, because of
certain speeches concerning God and the Holy City
which his contemporaries alleged were contrary to
the law.

2. The Jewish Mishna (the first part of the Tal-
mud) states that Manasseh slew Isaiah. Justin
Martyr (150 A. D.), in his controversial dialogue
with the Jew, Trypho, reproaches the Jews with
the accusation, " whom ye sawed asunder with a
wooden saw "; so also a Jewish Apocalypse of the
second century A. D., entitled " The Ascension of

Isaiah "; and likewise Epiphanius in his so-called
" Lives of the Prophets." It is possible that there
is an allusion to Isaiah's martyrdom in Heb. 11:
37, " they were stoned, they were sawn asunder,"
but this is by no means certain.

3. In any case Isaiah probably survived the great
catastrophe of the siege of Jerusalem in 701 B. C.,
and possibly also the death of Hezekiah (699
B. C.); for in 2 Chron. 32: 32 it is stated that Isaiah
wrote a biography of King Hezekiah. If so, his
prophetic activity extended over a period of more
than forty years. George Adam Smith extends it
to " more than fifty." (*Jerusalem*, vol. II., p. 180;
cf. Whitehouse, *Isaiah*, in the New Century Bible,
vol. I., p. 72).

Selected Literature

1. *Commentaries on Isaiah:* Whitehouse, in the
New Century Bible, 2 vols., 1905; Skinner, in the
Cambridge Bible for Schools and Colleges, 2 vols.,
1896; G. A. Smith, in the Expositor's Bible, 2 vols.,
1888-90; Delitzsch's Commentary, English edition,
2 vols., 1892; Cheyne's Commentary, third edition,
2 vols., 1884; Orelli's Commentary, translated by
Banks, 1895; Maclaren's Expositions of Holy Scripture, 2 vols., 1906. John E. McFadyen, the Bible
for Home and School, 1910. David Barton, The
Servant of Jehovah, 1922. Reuben Levy, Deutero-
Isaiah, 1925. Charles C. Torrey, The Second Isaiah, 1928.

2. *Introduction and Criticism:* Driver, Isaiah,
his Life and Times, in The Men of the Bible Series,
1888; Cheyne, Introduction to the Book of Isaiah,
1895; W. R. Smith, The Prophets of Israel, second
edition, 1896; Kirkpatrick, The Doctrine of the
Prophets, 1892; Thirtle, Old Testament Problems,
1907; König, The Exiles' Book of Consolation,
1899; Kennedy, The Arguments for the Unity of
Isaiah, 1891; Workman, The Servant of Jehovah,
1907; W. E. Barnes, An Examination of Isaiah,
24-27, 1891.

3. *Bible Dictionaries* (articles on " Isaiah ") : G. A. Smith, in Hastings' Dictionary of the Bible, 1899; Cheyne, in the Encyclopædia Biblica, 1901; James Robertson, in the Illustrated Bible Dictionary, 1908; König, in the Standard Bible Dictionary, 1909; G. B. Gray, in Hastings' (one volume) Dictionary of the Bible, 1909.

4. *In German:* the commentaries of Dillmann, 1890; Duhm, 1902; Marti, 1900; and Dillmann's as revised by Kittel, 1898, are recommended.

I, Even I, am He That Blotteth Out Thy Transgressions for Mine Own Sake; and I will not Remember Thy Sins.

Isa. 43: 25.

Look unto Me, and be Ye Saved, All the Ends of the Earth; for I am God, and There is None Else.
Isa. 45: 22.

STUDY TWO

ANALYSIS OF THE BOOK OF ISAIAH

The Six General Divisions of the Book

1. Chapters 1-12, prophecies concerning Judah and Jerusalem, closing with promises of restoration and a psalm of thanksgiving.

2. Chapters 13-23, oracles of judgment and salvation, for the most part concerning those foreign nations whose fortunes affected Judah and Jerusalem.

3. Chapters 24-27, Jehovah's world-judgment, issuing in the redemption of Israel.

4. Chapters 28-35, a cycle of prophetic warnings against alliance with Egypt, closing with a prophecy concerning Edom and a promise of Israel's ransom.

5. Chapters 36-39, history, prophecy and song intermingled; serving both as an appendix to chapters 1-35, and as an introduction to chapters 40-66.

6. Chapters 40-66, prophecies of comfort, salvation, and of the future glory awaiting Israel.

(The student would do well to mark off in some way these six divisions in his Bible; perhaps adding the headings in the margin.)

Chapters 1-12. Prophecies Concerning Judah and Jerusalem

Chapter 1. Jehovah's lament over Israel; an introduction striking the chief notes of the entire book: (1) thoughtlessness, verses 2-9; (2) formalism, verses 10-17; (3) pardon, verses 18-23; (4) redemption, verses 24-31.

Chapters 2-4. Three pictures of Zion: (1) her

future exaltation, 2: 2-4; (2) her present idolatry, 2: 5—4: 1; (3) her eventual purification, 4: 2-6.

Chapter 5. Isaiah's arraignment of Judah and Jerusalem: (1) parable of the vineyard, verses 1-7; (2) a series of six woes, verses 8-23; (3) first description of the Assyrian invaders, verses 24-30.

Chapter 6. The prophet's inaugural vision and commission.

Chapters 7: 1—9: 7. The prophecy of Immanuel; history and prediction being intermingled.

Chapters 9: 8—10: 4. An announcement to North Israel of impending ruin, with a refrain (9: 13, 17, 21; 10: 4).

Chapter 10: 5-34. Assyria, the rod of Jehovah's anger.

Chapter 11: 1-9. The Messianic reign of ideal peace.

Chapter 11: 10-16. The return of Israel and Judah from exile; no more any rivalry between them.

Chapter 12. A thanksgiving psalm of the redeemed nation.

(The student should also designate in some way these subdivisions in the text of his Bible.)

Chapters 13-23. Oracles of Judgment and Salvation, for the most part Concerning those Foreign Nations whose Fortunes Affected Judah and Jerusalem

Chapters 13: 2—14: 23. The downfall of Babylon: (1) judgment upon the city, 13: 2-22; (2) judgment upon the king, 14: 1-23.

Chapter 14: 24-27. The certain destruction of the Assyrian.

Chapter 14: 28-32. An oracle concerning Philistia.

Chapters 15-16. An oracle concerning Moab.

Chapter 17: 1-11.   An oracle concerning Damascus and North Israel.

Chapter 17: 12-14.   The annihilation of Judah's enemies.

Chapter 18.   A prediction concerning Ethiopia.

Chapter 19.   An oracle concerning Egypt.

Chapter 20.   Sargon's march against Egypt and Ethiopia.

Chapter 21: 1-10.   An oracle concerning " the wilderness of the sea " (Babylon).

Chapter 21: 11-12.   An oracle concerning Seir (Edom).

Chapter 21: 13-17.   An oracle concerning Arabia.

Chapter 22: 1-14.   An oracle " of the valley of vision " (Jerusalem).

Chapter 22: 15-25.   A philippic against Shebna, the comptroller of the palace.

Chapter 23.   An oracle concerning Tyre.

(The student should continue to designate in his Bible these main subdivisions; also those which follow.)

Chapters 24-27. Jehovah's World-Judgment, issuing in the Redemption of Israel

Chapter 24: 1-13.   Desolation of " the earth " and of " the city " (i. e., Judah and her towns).

Chapter 24: 14, 15.   The dawn of a better day.

Chapter 24: 16-23.   Premature songs of rejoicing; more judgment is coming.

Chapter 25: 1-5.   A hymn of thanksgiving, in which the prophet pleads for his people's deliverance.

Chapter 25: 6-8.   " A feast of fat things " to all nations " in this mountain," when death and the sorrows of war have passed away.

Chapter 25: 9-12. A second hymn of thanksgiving, looking to the time when Jehovah, the long looked-for deliverer, will come, and Moab's arrogance shall be laid low.

Chapter 26: 1-19. A third hymn of thanksgiving, because the "strong city" (Jerusalem) has been redeemed, and life has issued from the dead.

Chapters 26: 20—27: 1. An exhortation to God's people to hide themselves till God's judgment has shattered the world-powers.

Chapter 27: 2-6. A fourth hymn of thanksgiving, because deliverance from the enemy will be followed by national expansion.

Chapter 27: 7-11. Jehovah's discipline of Jacob has been for his good; the nations, on the contrary, have been punished and destroyed.

Chapter 27: 12, 13. The children of Israel shall be gathered from Assyria and from Egypt to worship Jehovah in Jerusalem.

Chapters 28-35. A Cycle of Prophetic Warnings against Alliance with Egypt, closing with a Prophecy Concerning Edom and a Promise of Israel's Ransom

Chapter 28: 1-6. The warning from Samaria.

Chapter 28: 7-22. The fate of the scoffing, dissolute politicians of Jerusalem.

Chapter 28: 23-29. A parable of comfort; God's judgments always proportionate to man's offense.

Chapter 29: 1-8. Jerusalem's humiliation and subsequent deliverance.

Chapter 29: 9-14. The people's spiritual stupidity.

Chapter 29: 15-24. Exposure of a conspiracy

with Egypt, followed by a graphic prediction of the ideal future.

Chapter 30: 1-17. An emphatic denunciation of the alliance with Egypt.

Chapter 30: 18-26. A brilliant picture of the Messianic age.

Chapter 30: 27-33. Jehovah's vengeance upon the Assyrian.

Chapter 31. The folly of relying on Egypt; Jehovah will protect Jerusalem and utterly destroy the Assyrian.

Chapter 32: 1-8. Another vivid picture of the Messianic age.

Chapter 32: 9-14. A rebuke to the women of Jerusalem.

Chapter 32: 15-20. The blessedness of the Messianic future.

Chapter 33. A woe pronounced upon an unnamed invader, followed by a promise of deliverance and the perfection of the kingdom of God.

Chapter 34. Jehovah's indignation against all nations, specially Edom.

Chapter 35. The future blessedness of the ransomed exiles.

Chapters 36-39. History, Prophecy and Song Intermingled; serving both as an Appendix to Chapters 1-35 and as an Introduction to Chapters 40-66

Chapter 36: 1 (2 Kings 18: 13). Sennacherib's invasion of Judah and capture of all her fortified cities.

Chapters 36: 2—37: 8 (2 Kings 18: 17—19: 8). Sennacherib sends Rabshakeh from Lachish against Hezekiah; Rabshakeh makes a defiant threat, but is unable to take Jerusalem.

Chapter 37: 9-38 (2 Kings 19: 9-37). Sennacherib suddenly threatened by Tirhakah, king of Ethiopia, sends messengers from Libnah to Hezekiah with a letter, peremptorily demanding the surrender of Jerusalem (vs. 9-13); Hezekiah spreads the letter before Jehovah in the temple and prays to be saved from the king of Assyria (vs. 14-20); Isaiah addresses to Hezekiah a prophecy predicting deliverance (vs. 21-35); Sennacherib's army is mysteriously destroyed, whereupon he returns to Nineveh and is subsequently assassinated by his sons (vs. 36-38).

Chapter 38: 1-8. Hezekiah's sickness, with the sign and promise of his recovery.

Chapter 38: 9-20. Hezekiah's song of thanksgiving.

Chapter 38: 21, 22. The means by which Hezekiah's cure is brought about.

Chapter 39. The embassy of Merodach-Baladan to Hezekiah.

Chapters 40-66. Prophecies of Comfort, Salvation and the Future Glory awaiting Israel

Chapters 40-48. Deliverance from captivity through Cyrus, promised by the infinite and incomparable Jehovah.

Chapters 49-57. The sufferings of the Servant of Jehovah; this section ending like the former with the refrain, " There is no peace, saith my God, to the wicked " (57: 21; cf. 48: 22).

Chapters 58-66. The abolition of all national distinctions and the future glory of the people of God. Chapter 60 is the characteristic chapter of this section, as chapter 53 is of the second, and chapter 40 of the first.

The great texts of Isaiah: 1: 3, 18; 2: 4; 6: 3, 8; 7: 14; 9: 6; 11: 6, 9; 12: 3; 21: 11, 12; 26: 3; 28: 10, 16, 20; 32: 2; 33: 14, 17; 35: 1, 10; 38: 1, 15, 16; 40: 1, 3, 8, 31; 42: 3, 21; 43 : 25; 45: 22; 52: 7; 53: 5; 54: 10; 55: 1, 6, 7; 59: 1; 60: 1, 8; 61: 1-3; 63: 1, 16; 65: 17; 66: 13.

THE OX KNOWETH HIS OWNER, AND THE ASS HIS MASTER'S CRIB; BUT ISRAEL DOTH NOT KNOW, MY PEOPLE DOTH NOT CONSIDER.

ISA. 1: 3.

FOR JERUSALEM IS RUINED, AND JUDAH IS FALLEN; BECAUSE THEIR TONGUE AND THEIR DOINGS ARE AGAINST JEHOVAH, TO PROVOKE THE EYES OF HIS GLORY.

ISA. 3: 8.

OH THAT THOU HADST HEARKENED TO MY COMMANDMENTS! THEN HAD THY PEACE BEEN AS A RIVER, AND THY RIGHTEOUSNESS AS THE WAVES OF THE SEA.

ISA. 48: 18.

STUDY THREE

THE PERIOD OF ISAIAH

Under Uzziah; Prior to His Call (740 B.C.)

1. According to the title of his book (1: 1), Isaiah prophesied during the reigns of Uzziah, Jotham, Ahaz, and Hezekiah, kings of Judah, or ca. 740-701 B. C. He dates his inaugural vision (6: 1) in Uzziah's death year (740 B. C.). As the prophet seems to have possessed the judgment and influence of a mature man from the beginning of his active ministry, it may be safely assumed that he was born as early as 765 B. C., or about the middle of Uzziah's long and prosperous reign (789-740 B. C.).

2. As a young man Isaiah witnessed the rapid development of Judah into a strong commercial and military state; for under Uzziah Judah attained a degree of prosperity and strength never before enjoyed since the days of Solomon. Walls, towers, fortifications, a large standing army, a port for commerce on the Red Sea, increased inland trade, tribute from the Ammonites, success in war with the Philistines and the Arabians—all these were Judah's during Uzziah's long reign (2 Kings 14: 22; 2 Chron. 26).

3. But along with power and wealth and luxury came also the sins of avarice, oppression, religious formality, and corruption. Jerusalem became not only populous but cosmopolitan. The temple revenues indeed were greatly increased, but religion and life were too frequently dissociated; the nation's progress was altogether material.

4. On the other hand all the surrounding nations were correspondingly weak, excepting North Israel under Jeroboam II. (784-745 B. C.), in which

also opulence and unusual prosperity prevailed; for Israel, like Persia, and in more modern times Spain before the destruction of the Armada, was most prosperous just before the nation's final collapse.

During the Reign of Jotham (740-736 B.C.)

1. Jotham for several years was probably associated with his father Uzziah as co-regent, because of the latter's leprosy (2 Kings 15: 5). In 740 B. C., however, he became sole king, continuing his father's policy of building and fortifying the capital (2 Kings 15: 35; 2 Chron. 27: 3).

2. But a new power was about to break over the eastern horizon. The Assyrians, with whom Ahab had come into contact at the battle of Karkar in 854 B. C., and to whom Jehu had paid tribute in 842 B. C., began to manifest anew their characteristic lust of conquest.

3. Tiglath-pileser III. (the same as " Pul " of 2 Kings 15: 19), a born general and a statesman, inaugurated a new epoch in Assyrian history. He reigned from 745 to 727 B. C. The first three years of his reign were spent in subduing the Armenians and Medes in the north and east. He then turned his attention westward; in 738 B. C., Arpad, Calno, Carchemish, Hamath and Damascus were reduced and made to pay tribute. Likewise Menahem, king of Israel (745-737 B. C.), following the ignoble example of Jehu, hastened to purchase vassalage at a price amounting to about two millions of dollars (2 Kings 15: 19). This short-sighted policy of seeking to buy the friendship of Assyria led to an outbreak of patriotism on the part of Menahem's subjects. Pekah, Menahem's chief general, became the leader of what might be called the patriotic party, and eventually found his way to the throne.

THE PERIOD OF ISAIAH

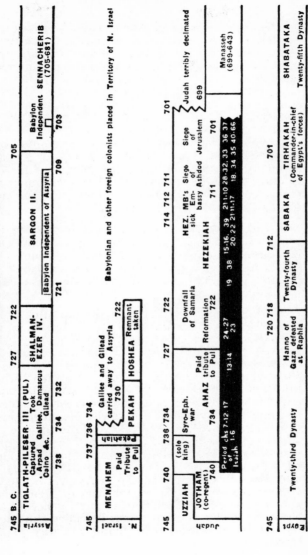

During the Reign of Ahaz (736-727 B.C.)

1. The presence of Tiglath-pileser in the west (738 B. C.) had led Pekah, the new king of North Israel (736-730 B. C.), and Rezin, king of Damascus, to form an alliance, in order to resist further encroachment on the part of Assyria. When Ahaz of Jerusalem (736-727 B. C.) refused to join their confederacy they resolved to dethrone him and set in his stead the son of Tabeel upon the throne of David (2 Kings 16: 5; Isa. 7: 6). The Edomites and Philistines also made frequent inroads into Judah about this time (2 Chron. 28: 17-18).

2. The struggle which ensued is commonly known as the Syro-Ephraimitic war (734 B. C.)— one of the greatest events in Isaiah's period. According to the chronicler, Judah was brought very low (2 Chron. 28: 19). Ahaz in panic sent to Tiglath-pileser for help (Isa. 7). The great Assyrian warrior of course responded with alacrity. He sacked Gaza and carried Galilee and Gilead into captivity (734 B. C.), and finally took Damascus (732 B. C.), besides receiving rich rewards from Ahaz (2 Kings 16: 7-9; 15: 29; Isa. 9: 1). On the same expedition Tiglath-pileser also exacted tribute from Ashkelon, Ammon, Moab, Edom, and the Arabians.

3. The religious as well as the political effect of Ahaz's policy was decidedly baneful. To please Tiglath-pileser Ahaz went to Damascus to join in the celebration of his victories, and while there saw a Syrian altar, a pattern of which he sent to Jerusalem and had a copy set up in the temple in place of the brazen altar of Solomon. Thus Ahaz, with all the influence of a king, introduced the religion of Syria into Jerusalem, even causing his sons to pass through the fire (2 Kings 16: 10-16; 2 Chron. 28).

Isaiah at this time was not far from thirty years of age.

During the Early Years of Hezekiah (727ff. B.C.)

1. Hezekiah came to the throne of Judah at the age of twenty-five and reigned twenty-nine years (727-699 B. C.). Isaiah was at least fifteen years his senior. The young king inherited from his father a very heavy burden. The splendor of Uzziah's and Jotham's reigns was rapidly fading before the menacing and ever avaricious Assyrians. Judah and Jerusalem had also received a shock in 734 B. C. when they beheld Tiglath-pileser carry at least two thirds of North Israel into captivity. Accordingly Hezekiah began his reign in Judah with a reformation. " He removed the high places and brake the pillars and cut down the Asherah " (2 Kings 18: 4, 22). He even invited the surviving remnant of North Israel to join in celebrating the Passover (2 Chron. 30).

2. But Israel's end was drawing near. Hoshea, the vacillating puppet-king of North Israel (730-722 B. C.), encouraged by Egypt, refused longer to pay Assyria his annual tribute (2 Kings 17: 4). Tiglath-pileser had died, but his son, Shalmaneser IV., who succeeded him (727-722 B. C.), promptly appeared before the gates of Samaria in 724 B. C. and for three weary years besieged the city (2 Kings 17: 5). Shalmaneser died just before the city capitulated; but his successor, Sargon II. (722-705 B. C.), records in his annals that during his first regnal year (722 B. C.) Samaria was actually captured, and 27,290 of Israel's choicest people deported to Assyria (2 Kings 17: 6); and further, that colonists were brought from Babylonia and other adjacent districts and placed in the cities of Samaria (2 Kings 17: 24).

3. Thus the kingdom of North Israel passed com-

pletely away and Judah was left ever after quite
exposed to the direct ravages, political and religious, of her Assyrio-Babylonian neighbors. Judah
herself barely escaped destruction by promising
heavy tribute to Assyria.

During Babylonia's Independence (721-709 B.C.)

1. Among the many vassal kinglets who rebelled
when Sargon seized the throne of Assyria in 722
B. C., there was one who proved too powerful to be
subdued, namely, Merodach-Baladan, the ever am-
bitious and irresistible patriot of Babylonia and
the uncompromising sworn enemy of Assyria. For
twelve years he maintained independent supremacy over Babylon (721-709 B. C.).

2. Sargon, accordingly, recognizing the impossibility of dislodging Merodach-Baladan from
Babylon, turned his attention toward Syria and
Palestine. In 720 B. C., at Karkar, he conquered
the recalcitrant kings of Arpad, Hamath and Damascus; then, entering Palestine, he defeated at
Raphia, Hanno of Gaza, and deposed Azuri, king
of Ashdod (720 B. C.). Judah, Moab and Edom
escaped by paying heavy toll. In 717 B. C., Sargon
added Carchemish, the capital of the Hittites, and
Media to his many victories.

3. In 714 B. C., Hezekiah fell desperately ill and,
being childless, was seriously concerned for the future of the Davidic dynasty. He resorted to prayer,
however, and God graciously extended his life fifteen years (2 Kings 20; Isa. 38). Whereupon
Merodach-Baladan, hearing of Hezekiah's wonderful cure, seized the opportunity of sending an embassy to Jerusalem to congratulate him on his recovery (712 B. C.), and at the same time probably
sought to form an alliance with Judah to resist
Assyrian supremacy. Hezekiah cordially received
the Babylonian ambassadors and foolishly showed

them all his treasures (2 Kings 20: 12-21; Isa. 39). Nothing came of the alliance, for the following year (711 B. C.) Sargon's army reappeared in Philistia in order to discipline Ashdod for similar conspiracy with the king of Egypt. Isaiah had now passed middle life.

During the Crisis of 701 B.C.

1. Judah and her neighbors groaned more and more under the heavy exactions of Assyria. Accordingly, when Sargon was assassinated and Sennacherib came to the throne (705 B. C.), rebellion broke out on all sides. Merodach-Baladan, who had been expelled by Sargon in 709 B. C., again took Babylon and held it for at least six months (703 B. C.). Hezekiah, who was encouraged by Egypt and all Philistia, except Padi of Ekron, the puppet-king of Sargon, refused longer to pay Assyria tribute (2 Kings 18: 7). Meanwhile a strong pro-Egyptian party had sprung up in Jerusalem.

2. Consequently in 701 B. C., Sennacherib marched westward with a vast army, sweeping everything before him. Tyre was invested though not taken; on the other hand, Joppa, Eltekeh, Ekron, Ashkelon, Ammon, Moab and Edom all promptly yielded to his demands. Hezekiah was panic-stricken and hastened to bring rich tribute, stripping even the temple and the palace of their treasures to do so (2 Kings 18: 13-16). But Sennacherib was not yet satisfied. He overran Judah, capturing, as he tells us in his inscription, forty-six walled towns and smaller villages without number, carrying 200,150 of Judah's population into captivity to Assyria, and demanding as tribute 800 talents of silver and thirty talents of gold (over $1,500,000); he took also Hezekiah's daughters and palace women, seized his male and female singers, and carried away enormous spoil.

3. But the end was not yet. Sennacherib himself, with the bulk of his army, halted to reduce

Lachish; thence he sent a strong detachment under Rabshakeh to besiege Jerusalem (2 Kings 18: 17—19: 8; Isa. 36: 2—37: 8). As he expresses it in his own inscription, " I shut up Hezekiah in Jerusalem like a bird in a cage." Rabshakeh, the commander-in-chief, failed, however, to capture the city and returned to Sennacherib, who meanwhile had conquered Lachish and was now warring against Libnah.

4. A second expedition against Jerusalem was planned; but hearing that Tirhakah (at that time the commander-in-chief of Egypt's forces and only afterwards " king of Ethiopia ") was approaching, Sennacherib sent messengers with a letter to Hezekiah, demanding immediate surrender of the city (2 Kings 19: 9-37; Isa. 37: 9-38). Hezekiah, however, through Isaiah's influence held out; and in due time, though Sennacherib disposed of Tirhakah's army without difficulty, his immense host in some mysterious way—by plague or otherwise—was suddenly smitten, and the great Assyrian conqueror was forced to return to Nineveh, possibly because Merodach-Baladan had again appeared in Babylonia. Sennacherib never again returned to Palestine, so far as we know, during the subsequent twenty years of his reign (705-681 B. C.), though he did make an independent expedition into North Arabia (691-689 B. C.).

5. This invasion of Judah by Sennacherib in 701 B. C. was *the* great event in Isaiah's ministry. Had it not been for the prophet's statesmanship, Jerusalem might have capitulated. As it was, only a small remnant of Judah's population escaped. Isaiah was now well-nigh sixty-five years of age, having preached full forty years. How much longer he labored is not known.

The Most Noteworthy Facts of Isaiah's Period

1. The immense contrast between the Judah of

Isaiah's earlier and the Judah of his later years. Wealth and luxury, under Uzziah and Jotham; the country districts depopulated and the capital a mere shadow of its former self, after the siege by Sennacherib.

2. The complete overthrow of North Israel; and in its place a colony of Babylonians and other foreigners, mingling necessarily more or less with the people of Judah and manufacturing idols in Palestine as they had been wont to do at home (2 Kings 17: 29-33).

3. The social conditions which prevailed were almost hopeless. Great wealth and extreme poverty existed side by side. The rich oppressed the poor (cf. Mic. 2 and 3). The women were haughty and gaily attired (Isa. 3: 16ff.). Avarice, drunkenness, careless carousing, daring defiance and wrong-doing, apathy to moral distinctions, and self-conceit prevailed, especially among the politicians and judges who were expected to guard the nation's interests (Isa. 5: 8-23). The ravages of war greatly aggravated the woeful poverty of the country peasants.

4. Religion had become corrupt. Ahaz had introduced a Syrian altar, and with it a stream of idolatrous practices. Hezekiah's reforms were drastic, but only temporary. The newly settled colonists from Babylonia and other places, in the territory which once belonged to North Israel, increased the tendency to idolatry. Soothsaying, incantations and necromancy took the place of loyalty to Jehovah, who seemed to have forsaken Israel (Isa. 2: 6; 8: 19, 20; 28: 18; 65: 4). Prophets and priests had degenerated (Isa. 28: 7); religion and morality had become almost utterly divorced (Isa. 1: 5-16); even the chief representative of the house of David, Ahaz the king, made his sons pass through the fire. Under such conditions and to such an age Isaiah was called to preach.

Chronological Table

B.C., ca. 765.	Isaiah born.
789-740.	Uzziah.
784-745.	Jeroboam II.
745-727.	Tiglath-pileser III.
740.	The Call of Isaiah.
740-736.	Jotham (sole reign).
738.	Arpad, Calno, Carchemish and Damascus taken by Tiglath-pileser III.
745-737.	Menahem.
737-736.	Pekahiah.
736-730.	Pekah
736-727.	Ahaz.
734.	Syro-Ephraimitic war; Gaza captured by Tiglath-pileser III.; Galilee and Gilead also carried captive to Assyria.
732.	Damascus taken by Tiglath-pileser III.
730-722.	Hoshea.
727-699.	Hezekiah.
727-722.	Shalmaneser IV.
722.	Fall of Samaria; end of the kingdom of North Israel.
722-705.	Sargon II.
721-709.	Babylonia independent under Merodach-Baladan.
720.	Battle of Karkar; Sargon II. conquers Arpad, Hamath and Damascus. Battle of Raphia; Sargon II. conquers Hanno of Gaza; King So of Egypt flees.
717.	Sargon II. conquers the Hittites, capturing Carchemish, their capital; annexing also Media to his empire.
714.	Hezekiah's sickness.
712.	Merodach-Baladan's embassy to Hezekiah.
712-700.	Shabaka, founder of twenty-fifth dynasty in Egypt.
711.	Siege of Ashdod by Sargon II.
709.	Merodach-Baladan expelled from Babylonia by Sargon II.

705-681.   Sennacherib.

703.   Merodach-Baladan again king (six months) over Babylonia.

701.   Siege of Jerusalem by Sennacherib; Judah, Moab, Edom, Ammon and Philistia made to pay tribute. Tirhakah (afterwards "king of Ethiopia") head of the Egyptian army under Shabaka.

699-643.   Manasseh, king of Judah.

THE WILDERNESS AND THE DRY LAND SHALL BE GLAD;
AND THE DESERT SHALL REJOICE, AND BLOSSOM AS THE
ROSE.

ISA. 35: 1.

AND A HIGHWAY SHALL BE THERE, AND IT SHALL BE
CALLED, THE WAY OF HOLINESS; THE UNCLEAN SHALL
NOT PASS OVER IT; BUT IT SHALL BE FOR THE REDEEMED:
THE WAYFARING MEN, YEA, FOOLS, SHALL NOT ERR
THEREIN.

ISA. 35: 8.

AND THE RANSOMED OF JEHOVAH SHALL RETURN, AND
COME WITH SINGING UNTO ZION; AND EVERLASTING JOY
SHALL BE UPON THEIR HEADS: THEY SHALL OBTAIN
GLADNESS AND JOY, AND SORROW AND SIGHING SHALL
FLEE AWAY.

ISA. 35: 10; 51: 11.

STUDY FOUR

ISAIAH'S PROPHECIES CHRONOLOGICALLY ARRANGED

The Inner Structure of His Book

1. The editorial arrangement of Isaiah's prophecies is very suggestive. In the main they stand in chronological order. All the *dates* mentioned are in strict historical sequence; for example, 6: 1, "in the year that king Uzziah died " (740 B. C.); 7: 1, " in the days of Ahaz " (735ff. B. C.); 14: 28, " in the year that king Ahaz died " (727 B. C.); 20: 1, " in the year that Tartan came unto Ashdod, when Sargon the king of Assyria sent him " (711 B. C.); 36: 1, " in the fourteenth year of king Hezekiah " (701 B. C.). These points are all in strict chronological order.

2. Isaiah's great individual messages are also arranged in true historical sequence; thus, chapters 1-6 for the most part belong to the last years of Jotham's reign (740-736 B. C.); chapters 7-12, to the period of the Syro-Ephraimitic war (734 B. C.); chapter 20, to the year of Sargon's siege of Ashdod (711 B. C.); chapters 28-32, to the invasion of Judah by Sennacherib (701 B. C.); while the distinctively promissory portions (chapters 40-66), as is natural, conclude the collection.

3. In several instances, however, there are notable departures from a rigid chronological order. For example, chapter 6, which describes the prophet's initial call to preach, follows the rebukes and denunciations of chapters 1-5; but this is probably due to its being used by the prophet as an apologetic. Having pronounced "woes" upon others (5: 8-23), he pauses to assure his hearers that he first pronounced " woe " upon himself (6: 5).

4. Again, the oracles against foreign nations in chapters 13-23, though belonging to various dates, are grouped together. This is doubtless due, to some extent at least, to their subject matter. Like-

wise, chapters 38-39, which give an account of
Hezekiah's sickness and Merodach-Baladan's embassy to him (714-712 B. C.), chronologically precede chapters 36-37, which describe Sennacherib's
investment of Jerusalem (701 B. C.). This order,
however, is due probably to the desire to make
chapters 36-37 (about Sennacherib) an appropriate
conclusion to chapters 1-35 (which are chiefly
about Assyria), and on the other hand, to make
chapters 38-39 (about Merodach-Baladan) a suitable introduction to chapters 40-66 (which speak
of Babylon).

Isaiah's Earliest Messages (Chapters 1-6)

1. The attempt to date Isaiah's individual prophecies, on the basis of internal criteria alone, is a
well-nigh impossible task; and yet no other evidence is available. Oftentimes passages stand side
by side which point in opposite directions; in fact,
certain sections seem to be composed of various
fragments dating from different periods, as though
prophecies widely separated from each other in
time had been fused together. In such cases much
weight should be given to those features which
point to an early origin, because of the predominatingly predictive character of Isaiah's writings.
Isaiah always had an eye upon the future. His
semi-historical and biographical prophecies are
naturally the easiest to date; on the other hand,
the form of his Messianic and eschatological discourses is largely due to his own personal temper
and psychology, rather than to the historical circumstances of the time. Fortunately, the exact
dating of any given prophecy while a desideratum
is not absolutely essential.

2. Chapters 1-6, barring certain unimportant
editorial additions, are probably Isaiah's earliest
messages to Judah and Jerusalem, dating from the
reign of Jotham (740-736 B. C.). They breathe the
atmosphere of Jotham's period; prosperity and
abundance (2: 7), elaborate sacrifices (1: 11), ex-

travagant dress and ostentation (3: 16-24), excessive indulgence in wine and strong drink, avarice and self-confidence (5: 8-23). The interspersed descriptions of desolation (1: 7), ruin (3: 8), captivity (5: 13), and of a remnant (6: 13), on the other hand, are anticipatory of impending issues which the prophet at this very early period of his ministry foresaw. The prophet often fused " the actual present with the expected future "; always speaking as a poet in the elevated style of a seer; seeing the issues of cause and effect even before Jehovah began to send enemies against Judah (2 Kings 15: 37).

Prophecies in Connection with the Syro-Ephraimitic War of 734 B.C. (Chapters 7-12; 17)

1. Some of Isaiah's most powerful messages were inspired by the circumstances of the crisis in 734 B. C., when Pekah of Israel and Rezin of Damascus came up against Jerusalem and threatened to dethrone King Ahaz because he refused to ally himself with them against Assyria. Chapters 7-12 and 17 seem to belong, for the most part, to this date.

2. Ahaz, youthful and inexperienced, is on the point of sending to Assyria for help against his foes to the north (2 Kings 16: 7), when Isaiah, at the bidding of Jehovah, approaches to remonstrate with him against a policy so obviously suicidal (7: 1—9: 7). Isaiah thus appears in the new role of a practical statesman, warning the king against the short-sighted policy of making friends with Assyria, and urging that he put his trust in Jehovah.

3. Chapters 9: 8—10: 4 also belong to this period; warning Ephraim of the sure consequences of arrogance, which will lead to fire-devouring anarchy.

4. Chapter 10: 5-34 predicts the ultimate downfall of the proud Assyrian, who is but the "rod"

of divine wrath (after 734 B. C.). This is followed
by a Messianic passage of comfort in chapter 11, in
which the prophet promises a return of the exiles,
" from the four corners of the earth," and a second
exodus " after the manner of Egypt." The references to Egypt in 10: 24, 26 and 11: 15, 16 would
hardly be as natural after the rise of a strong Egyptian party in Jerusalem, such as existed in the latter years of Hezekiah; and 11: 13 certainly points
in the direction of 734 B. C. Chapter 12 is an ode
of thanksgiving put by the prophet into the mouth
of the redeemed remnant, and most fittingly concludes the Messianic picture of chapter 11.

5. Chapter 17, which deals with the outcome of
the war in its effects upon Syria and Ephraim,
only " gleanings " being left (v. 6), belongs also to
this crisis; the oracle closes, like 9: 8—10: 4, with
an announcement that Assyria, the despoiler, will
in turn be despoiled himself (vs. 12-14).

Prophecies between 734 and 722 B.C.
(Chapters 13-14 and 23-27)

1. Modern expositors usually regard the prophet's years between 734 and 722 B. C. as years of in-
activity, assigning to this period no prophecies at
all, or at most only a few verses. But it seems
quite improbable that a prophet of Isaiah's type
should have remained inactive during such a critical period. On the contrary, it may safely be assumed that he improved these years in training
and instructing his " disciples."

2. In his earlier utterances (11: 11, 12) he had
made mention of foreign nations such as Philistia,
Edom, Moab, Ammon, and the Arabians; he now
addresses to them individual messages after the
tenor of chapter 2: 2-4, with all the severity of an
Amos (chapters 1-2), the tenderness of a Jeremiah
(chapters 47-51), and the vision of an Ezekiel
(chapters 25-32). These he probably committed to
the custody of his own inner circle.

3. The first prophecy to spring out of the events of 734-732 B. C., when Tiglath-pileser stripped Israel of Gilead and Galilee, and captured Damascus, is the much disputed prophecy in 13: 2—14: 23, whose title reads, " The burden of Babylon, which Isaiah the son of Amoz did see." Following it, there is a brief prophecy which explicitly mentions " Assyria " as the object of Jehovah's destruction (14: 24-27). The title of chapters 13-14, therefore, as in the case of chapter 17, is hardly expressive of the oracle's true scope; chapters 13-14 are really directed against both Babylonia and Assyria; and it is acknowledged now even by Winckler and Cheyne that no *Babylonian* king answers the description of 14: 4ff.

4. The prophecy against Philistia (14: 28-32) bears the very appropriate title, " In the year that king Ahaz died " (727 B. C.). In this oracle the prophet rebukes Philistia for rejoicing over the death of Tiglath-pileser, who, as Jehovah's "rod," had smitten her.

5. Isaiah's vision in these early years probably extended further (chapters 24-27). Isaiah sees that before Assyria is destroyed she will be used of Jehovah to bring desolation, not only to Syria and Israel, but to the whole land (24: 3). Cities will fall (24: 12; 25: 2), Moab will be trodden down (25: 10), and the remnant of the nation will come from Assyria and Egypt (27: 13), while in Mount Zion Jehovah will make a feast of fat things unto all nations (25: 6). Chapters 24-27 contain this vision and, in the writer's judgment, are best explained as arising during the years just prior to 722 B. C.

6. The oracle against Tyre (chapter 23) seems to precede the great sweeping invasions made by Shalmaneser IV., Sargon II. and Sennacherib, and therefore belongs to this same period (before 722 B. C.).

During the Reign of Sargon II, 722-705 B.C.
(Chapters 15-16, 19-22, 38-39)

1. The oracle against Egypt (chapter 19) is best explained as arising out of the year 720 B. C., when Sargon humbled Egypt at Raphia. The prophet here draws a vivid picture of Egypt's political, material and social decay; but he also promises that she will be converted to Jehovah.

2. Chapters 38-39, which tell of Hezekiah's sickness and Merodach-Baladan's embassy of congratulation upon his recovery, belong most probably to the years 714 and 712 B. C., respectively.

3. The oracle against Moab (chapters 15-16) is best assigned to the period just preceding 711 B. C., when Sargon returned to Palestine, as he tells us, to punish " Philistia, Judah, Edom and Moab " for speaking treason. Possibly Isaiah had delivered the bulk of this oracle on a previous occasion, to which " now " he adds an important prediction (16: 13-14). Chapter 20 predicts Assyria's victory over Egypt and Ethiopia in 711 B. C.

4. The brief, enigmatical oracles against Seir (21: 11, 12) and Arabia (21: 13-17) probably belong to this same date, as Sargon received tribute from them in the year 711 B. C.; likewise the prophet's trenchant rebuke to the citizens of Jerusalem (22: 1-14) for their levity and indifferent abandon, while Sargon's troops were standing before Jerusalem's gates; and the prophecy concerning the deposition of Shebna from his position as comptroller of the palace (22: 15-25).

5. The oracle of " the wilderness of the sea," i. e., Babylon (21: 1-10), evidently describes the siege of Babylon in 709 B. C., when Sargon finally succeeded in rescuing the city from the indomitable usurper, Merodach-Baladan. Babylon's fate would especially interest Jerusalem if Hezekiah, as is probable, made an alliance in 712 B. C. with

Merodach-Baladan's embassy of congratulation to him upon his recovery from sickness.

Prior to and during the Siege of 701 B.C. (Chapters 28-37 and 18)

1. Chapters 28-32 (excepting verses 1-6 of chapter 28, which are earlier) clearly belong to the time shortly prior to 701 B. C. They record the prophet's earnest and oft repeated expostulations against the folly of depending on Egypt. They are frequently interspersed with gleams of hope for the remnant of Judah and brilliant pictures of the Messianic future. The Assyrian, on the contrary, will be utterly destroyed.

2. Chapter 18, containing a prophecy against Ethiopia, describes the terror in the Nile valley which Sennacherib produced by his approach in 701 B. C.

3. Chapter 33, one of the grandest of all Isaiah's prophecies, describes in advance the actual deliverance of Jerusalem in 701 B. C. Chapters 36-37 explain the historical steps by which the capital became invested and was eventually delivered, containing a prophecy by Isaiah (37: 22-35) in which Jerusalem proudly mocks her arrogant assailants who are so soon to go down before the angel of Jehovah.

4. Chapters 34-35 are a proclamation to the nations to behold the spectacle of Assyria's overwhelming defeat. So shall all Zion's enemies perish; Edom in particular is doomed to perpetual ruin and solitude. Israel's lot, on the contrary, will be one of happiness and everlasting joy.

After the Crisis of 701 B.C. (Chapters 40-66)

1. Through Jehovah's interposition Sennacherib was forced to return to Nineveh without actually

capturing Jerusalem. The merest remnant of the kingdom of Judah was left in the land. Sennacherib claims to have taken over 200,000 captives from Judah. Twenty years before, Sargon had transplanted the choicest of North Israel to the far East.

2. The time had „now come to comfort Zion (chapters 40-66). Primarily these wonderful prophecies were addressed to the remnant of Isaiah's own period, at home and scattered abroad. The history of criticism has demonstrated that no other *single* period in all of Israel's history so well accounts for their origin as the period of Isaiah; and to break them up into various fragments and deny their unity, is, as Dillmann characteristically remarks, " diseased reflection."

3. The prophet's standpoint in chapters 40-66 is that of Isaiah himself. For if Isaiah before 734 B. C., in passages confessedly his own, c⌒⸱'d describe Judah's cities as already " burn⸱⸱ with fire," Zion as deserted as " a booth in a vineyard " (1: 7, 8), Jerusalem as " ruined," Judah as " fallen " (3: 8), and Jehovah's people as already " gone into captivity " (5: 13), surely after all the destruction and devastation wrought on Judah by Assyria in the years 722, 720, 711, and 701 B. C., the same prophet with the same poetic license could declare that the temple had been "trodden down" (63: 18) and " burned with fire," and all Judah's pleasant places "laid waste" (64: 11); and, in perfect keeping with his former promises, could add that "they shall repair the waste cities, the desolations of many generations (61: 4, cf. 44: 26; 58: 12)

4. Or, again, if Isaiah the son of Amoz could comfort Jerusalem with promises of protection when the Assyrian (734 B. C.) should come like an overflowing river (8: 9, 10; 10: 24, 25), and conceive a beautiful parable of comfort like that contained in 28: 23-29, and insert among his warnings

and exhortations of that gloomy time (702 B. C.)
so many precious promises of a brighter future
which was sure to follow Sennacherib's invasion
(29: 17-24; 30: 29ff; 31: 8), and, in the very
midst of the siege, conceive of such marvelous Messianic visions as those in 33: 17-24 with which to
dispel the dismay of his compatriots; surely the
same prophet would probably seize the opportunity to comfort those of Zion who survived the
great catastrophe of 701 B. C. The prophet who
had done the one thing was prepared to do the
other.

5. But there was one circumstance of the prophet's position after 701 B. C. which was new, and
which he did not and indeed could not have employed as an argument in enforcing his messages
prior to the Assyrian's overthrow and Jerusalem's
deliverance, namely, the fulfilment of previous predictions. Over and over again in these last chapters Isaiah appeals to Jehovah's power to predict,
pointing victoriously to the fulfilment of former
predictions as a proof of Jehovah's deity.

6. From such passages we obtain an idea of the
prophet's true historical position (42: 9; 44: 8;
45: 21; 46: 10; 48: 3). Old predictions have already been fulfilled (6: 11-13; 29: 5; 30: 31; 31:
8; 37: 7, 30), on the basis of which the prophet
ventures to predict new and even more astounding
things concerning the overthrow of Babylon by
Cyrus, and Israel's return from exile (43: 6).
Isaiah's book is signally full of predictions (7: 8,
16; 8: 4, 8; 9: 11, 12; 10: 26-34; 14: 24-27; 16:
14; 17: 9, 12-14; 20: 4-6; 21: 15-17; 22: 19ff.;
23: 15; 38: 5); some of which, written down and
sealed, were evidently committed by the prophet
to his inner circle of disciples to be used and veri-
fied by them in subsequent times (8: 16).

7. In view of these considerations, therefore,
and others which might be enumerated, the writer

ventures, at the risk of being reproached for undue conservatism, to assign chapters 40-66 to the period just following 701 B. C. as the most suitable historical background known.

THE GRASS WITHERETH, THE FLOWER FADETH; BUT THE WORD OF OUR GOD SHALL STAND FOREVER.

ISA. 40: 8.

FOR THE MOUNTAINS MAY DEPART, AND THE HILLS BE REMOVED; BUT MY LOVINGKINDNESS SHALL NOT DEPART FROM THEE, NEITHER SHALL MY COVENANT OF PEACE BE REMOVED, SAITH JEHOVAH THAT HATH MERCY ON THEE.

ISA. 54: 10.

AND ALL THY CHILDREN SHALL BE TAUGHT OF JEHOVAH; AND GREAT SHALL BE THE PEACE OF THY CHILDREN.

ISA. 54: 13.

STUDY FIVE

THE CRITICAL PROBLEM

The Status Questionis

1. " For nearly twenty-five centuries no one dreamt of doubting that Isaiah, the son of Amoz, was the author of every part of the book that goes under his name." (A. B. Davidson, *Old Testament Prophecy*, p. 244.) Recently, however, certain writers have appealed to 2 Chron. 36: 22ff. as external proof that Isa. 40-66 existed as a separate collection in the days of the chronicler (ca. 300 B. C.), but the evidence obtained from this source is so doubtful that it is well-nigh valueless.

2. Those who deny the integrity of the book may be divided into two groups, moderates and radicals. For the sake of setting forth as simply as possible the present state of the Isaiah problem, we will give in the first instance the chapters and verses which are commonly rejected by moderates as *non-Isaianic,* and in the second instance, the chapters and verses which are allowed even by radicals to be *the genuine prophecies of Isaiah.*

3. The moderate section of the critical school, which is best represented by Drs. Driver, G. A. Smith, Skinner, Kirkpatrick, König, A. B. Davidson, and Whitehouse, practically agrees that the following chapters and verses are *not Isaiah's:* 11: 10-16; 12: 1-6; 13: 1—14: 23; 15: 1—16:12; 21: 1-10; 24-27; 34-35; 36-39; 40-66. That is to say, some forty-four chapters out of the whole number, sixty-six, were *not* written by Isaiah.

4. The radical wing of the critical school, which is represented by Drs. Cheyne, Duhm, Gray, Hackmann, Guthe and Marti, rejects approximately 1030 verses out of the total 1292 in the book, retaining the following only as *the genuine product of Isaiah and his age:* 1: 2-26, 29-31; 2: 6-19; 3:

1, 5, 8, 9, 12-17, 24; 4: 1; 5: 1-14, 17-29; 6: 1-13;
7: 1—8: 22; 9: 8—10: 9; 10: 13, 14, 27-32; 14:
24-32; 17: 1-14; 18: 1-6; 20: 1-6; 22: 1-22; 28:
1-4, 7-22; 29: 1-6, 9, 10, 13-15; 30: 1-17; 31: 1-4.
That is, only about 262 verses out of the total 1292
are allowed to be genuine.

The Fundamental Axiom of Criticism

1. The fundamental principle which underlies
all modern criticism of Old Testament prophecy is
the twofold axiom or postulate that a prophet always spoke out of a definite historical situation
to the present needs of the people among whom he
lived; and that a definite historical situation shall
be pointed out for each prophecy.

2. This principle in general is sound; but it
must be accompanied with certain cautions equally
essential:

(1) Not every prophecy can be traced, independ-
ently of its context, to a definite historical situation
(cf. Joel 3; Zech. 9-14). Moreover, the prophets
often speak in poetry, and, therefore, in language
which should not be taken literally.

(2) It is not always the greatest event in a nation's history, or the event about which we in our
time happen to know the most, or even the event
which best fits the phraseology of any particular
prophecy, that may actually have given birth to it.
Israel's history was full of crises.

(3) While it is true that in the great majority
of cases the prophets spoke directly and practically
to the needs of their own generation, it is also true,
in the case of Isaiah at least, that the prophet commanded, "Bind thou up the testimony, seal the law
among my disciples " (8: 16), that is, *preserve my
teachings for the future.* Compare Isa. 30: 8, "Now

go, write it before them on a tablet, and inscribe it in a book, *that it may be for the time to come forever and ever;*" and 42: 23, " *hear for the time to come.*" As Paul's great doctrine of justification by faith was first discovered by Augustine and emphasized by Luther, so Isaiah obviously spoke words of comfort to his own generation which *to us* seem to have been directed primarily to the captives in Babylonian exile, but which may have been delivered to a much earlier generation. Thus the comforting messages of chapters 40-66 need not have been without great ethical and practical import to Isaiah's own contemporaries at the close of the eighth century B. C., while a century and a half later, also, they may have brought consolation to the Israelites in exiles. (For a discussion of "Cyrus" see Study Twelve.)

Other Governing Criteria

1. There are other governing criteria which lead some critics to reject various portions of Isaiah as subsequent to the prophet's own age. Only a few examples can be given by way of illustration:

(1) To one critic " the conversion of the heathen " lay quite beyond the horizon of any eighth century prophet and consequently Isa. 2: 2-4 and all similar passages should be relegated to a subsequent age.

(2) To another " the picture of universal peace" in Isa. 11: 1-9 is a symptom of a late date, and therefore the section must be deleted.

(3) To another the thought of universal judgment upon " the whole earth " in chapter 14: 26 quite transcends Isaiah's range of thought.

(4) To still another the apocalyptic character of chapters 24-27 represents a phase of Hebrew

thought which prevailed in Israel only after Ezekiel.

(5) Even to those who are considered moderates the poetic character of a passage like chapter 12 and the references to a return from captivity, as in 11: 11-16, and the promises and consolations such as are found in chapter 33, are cited as grounds for assigning these and kindred passages to a much later age. Radicals deny in toto the existence of Messianic passages in Isaiah's own prophecies.

2. But, to deny to Isaiah of the eighth century all catholicity of grace, all universalism of salvation, every highly developed Messianic ideal, every rich note of promise and comfort, all sublime faith in the sacrosanct character of Zion, as some do, is unwarrantably to create a new Isaiah of greatly reduced proportions, a mere preacher of inflexible righteousness, a statesman of not very optimistic vein, and the exponent of a cold ethical religion without the warmth and glow of the messages of salvation which characterize Isaiah, the prophet of the eighth century; if indeed he actually composed the book ascribed to him.

The Writer's Personal Attitude

1. More and more the writer is persuaded that broad facts must decide the unity or collective character of Isaiah's book. Verbal exegesis may do more harm than good. Greater regard must be paid to the *structure* of the book, which is no mere anthology, or collection of independent discourses by different writers belonging to different periods. There is an obvious, though it may be to some extent an editorial, unity to Isaiah's prophecies. To regard them as a heterogeneous mass of miscellaneous oracles which were written at widely

separated times and under varied circumstances from Isaiah's times down to the Maccabæan age, and revised and freely interpolated throughout the intervening centuries, is to lose sight of the great historic realities and perspective of the prophet.

2. Not in the spirit of an antiquated apologist, therefore, but rather as a contribution to historical criticism, the writer feels constrained to say, that to him chapter 2: 2-4 is the key to Isaiah's horizon; that chapters 40-66 are in germ wrapped up in the vision and commission of the prophet's inaugural call (chapter 6); and that the whole problem of how much or how little Isaiah wrote would become immensely simplified if critics would only divest themselves of a mass of unwarranted presuppositions and arbitrary restrictions which fix hard and fast what each century can think and say.

3. Accordingly, the writer's attitude is that of those who, while welcoming all ascertained results of investigation, decline to accept any mere conjectures or theories as final conclusions. And while he acknowledges his very great debt to critics of all latitudes, he nevertheless believes that the book of Isaiah, practically as we have it, may have been, and probably was, all written by Isaiah, the son of Amoz, in the latter half of the eighth century B. C. To what extent the editors revised and supplemented the prophet's discourses can never be definitely determined.

The History of Criticism

1. The critical disintegration of the book of Isaiah began with Koppe, who in 1780 first doubted the genuineness of chapter 50. Döderlein in 1789 expressed decided suspicion as to the Isaianic origin of the whole of chapters 40-66. He was followed by Rosenmüller, who was the first to deny

to Isaiah the prophecy against Babylon in chapters
13: 1—14: 23. Eichhorn at the beginning of the
last century further eliminated from the genuine
prophecies of Isaiah the oracle against Tyre in
chapter 23, and, with Gesenius and Ewald, denied
the Isaianic origin of chapters 24-27. Gesenius also
ascribed to some unknown prophet chapters 15
and 16. Rosenmüller went further, and pronounced against chapters 34 and 35; and not long
afterwards (1840), Ewald questioned chapters 12
and 33. Thus by the middle of the nineteenth century some thirty-seven or thirty-eight chapters
were rejected as no part of Isaiah's actual writings.

2. In 1879-80, the celebrated Leipzig professor,
Franz Delitzsch, who for years previous had de-
fended the genuineness of chapters 40-66, finally
yielded to the modern critical position, and in the
new edition of his commentary, published in 1889,
interpreted these chapters, though with considerable hesitation, as coming from the close of the
period of Babylonian exile. Shortly after this
(1888-90), Canon Driver and Dr. George Adam
Smith gave popular impetus to the new critical
position in Great Britain.

3. Since 1890, the criticism of Isaiah has been
more trenchant and microscopic than ever before.
Duhm, Stade, Guthe, Hackmann, Cornill and Marti
on the continent, and Cheyne, Gray and others in
Great Britain and America, have questioned portions which hitherto were supposed to be genuine;
rejecting, for example, all such promises of Messianic hope and salvation as are found in 2: 2-5;
4: 2-6; 9: 1-6; 11: 1-9.

4. On the other hand, there have not been wanting in all these years able defenders of the unity of
Isaiah's writings, e. g., Strachey (1874), Nagels-
bach (1877), Bredenkamp (1887), Barnes (1891),
Douglas (1895), W. H. Cobb (1883-1908), Green
(1892), Vos (1898-99), and Thirtle (1907), Mar-

goliouth (1910), Allis (1912), J. J. Lias (1915), and J. P. Wiles (1915); also J. Chaine (R. C.).

The Disintegration of "Deutero-Isaiah"

1. The unity of chapters 40-66 has likewise vanished in the hands of critics. What prior to 1890 was supposed to be the unique product of some celebrated but anonymous sage designated as "Deutero-Isaiah," who lived in Babylonia, is now commonly divided between a Deutero-Isaiah who wrote only chapters 40-55, and a Trito-Isaiah, who wrote most but not all of chapters 56-66.

2. At first it was thought sufficient to separate off chapters 63-66 as a later addition to the prophecies of Deutero-Isaiah; but more recently it has become the general fashion to distinguish between chapters 40-55, written in Babylonia (ca. 549-538 B. C.), and chapters 56-66, written in Palestine (ca. 460-445 B. C.).

3. But most radical critics carry disintegration considerably farther even than this, especially in the case of chapters 56-66, which are not considered a unity. For example, chapters 60, 61-62, 63: 7—64: 12 are extremely difficult to date; while chapters 56: 9—57: 21 confessedly describe conditions which suit better the idolatrous conditions of either pre-exilic or very late post-exilic times. Opinions also conflict as to where these prophecies were written, whether in Babylonia, Palestine, Phœnicia, or Egypt.

The Literary History of the Book

1. When or how the book of Isaiah was edited and brought into its present form is unknown. Jesus Ben-Sirach (Ecclesiasticus 48: 20-25), writing about 180 B. C., cites Isaiah as one of the no-

table worthies of Hebrew antiquity, in whose days
he says, " the sun went backward and he added
life to the king " (cf. Isa. 38: 4-8), and who " saw
by an excellent spirit that which should come to
pass at the last, and comforted them that mourned
in Zion " (cf. Isa. 40: 1; 61: 1-3; 41: 21-24; 43:
9-12; 44: 7-8; 46: 10-11; 48: 3-8). Evidently,
therefore, at the beginning of the second century
B. C., at the latest, the book of Isaiah had reached
its present form.

2. But there are signs of editorial work within
the book of Isaiah which were probably due to the
prophet himself: e. g., 8: 16, which points to a
definite collection of prophecies, perhaps chapters
2-6 (cf. 30: 8). The book seems to be made up of
many small collections, three of which have distinct titles of authorship (1: 1; 2: 1; 13: 1).

3. The prophet's " disciples " would naturally
edit his prophecies after his death. Only on some
such supposition can we account for chapters 2-6
and 13-23 being ascribed to Isaiah, whose name
must have been associated with these sections
from the very first.

4. On the other hand, there is absolutely no
proof that chapters 1-39, or any other considerable
section of his prophecies, ever existed by themselves as an independent collection; nor is there
any ground for thinking, as some allege, that the
promissory and Messianic portions have been sys-
tematically interpolated by editors long subsequent
to the prophet's own time. For promise and comfort are not wanting from the two confessedly
genuine portions in which Isaiah, using the first
person, gives snatches of his own biography (6: 1-
13; 8: 1-8).

Come Now, and Let Us Reason Together, Saith Jehovah: Though Your Sins be as Scarlet, They Shall be as White as Snow; Though They be Red Like Crimson, They Shall be as Wool.

Isa. 1: 18.

And He will Judge between the Nations, and will Decide Concerning Many Peoples; and They Shall Beat Their Swords into Plowshares, and Their Spears into Pruning Hooks; Nation Shall not Lift up Sword Against Nation, neither Shall They Learn War any More.

Isa. 2: 4.

STUDY SIX

JUDAH'S SOCIAL SINS (CHAPTERS 1-6)

Formal Religion (Chapter 1)

1. The dramatic discourse in chapter 1 contains a summary of all Isaiah's characteristic and essential teachings; and, therefore, is marvelously appropriate as an introduction to his book.

2. It is one of the earliest of Isaiah's prophecies, dating probably from the reign of Jotham, when Syria and North Israel began to threaten Judah in 736 B. C. (cf. 2 Kings 15: 37).

3. After the editorial title in v. 1, Isaiah describes the hopeless moral and religious condition of the nation (vs. 2-20), and the need of a purifying judgment (vs. 21-31).

4. Judah's sins are set forth as primarily and fundamentally sins of religion. She has rebelled against God (v. 2). The whole nation is insensible to God's goodness. Conscience is asleep: " My people do not think " (v. 3); yet they keep up the hollow forms of ritual sacrifice (vs. 11, 12). A bad conscience easily resorts to hollow worship.

5. The prophet bids them reform (vs. 16, 17); he even offers them gracious pardon (v. 18). But they remain stubborn and rebellious; accordingly he sings a dirge over Jerusalem in dirge meter (vs. 21-26), and warns them of approaching judgment: sin, he says, withers (v. 30); sin burns (v. 31).

6. The paramount lessons of the discourse are the too oft-forgotten facts that true religion is the prime condition of a healthy social order; that irreligion or formal ritual is a social vice; that no

man liveth to himself; and that what a peasant or
a prince believes is of public concern to all.

7. All social evils are traceable ultimately to rebellion against God.

The Sin of War (Chapter 2:1-4)

1. War was imminent when the prophet wrote
the well-known passage contained in 2: 2-4 (736
B. C.).   Probably Pekah of Israel and Rezin of Damascus were already planning to strike a death
blow at Jerusalem.

2. This same inspired vision has also been incor-
porated by the collectors of prophecy among the
writings of Isaiah's younger contemporary, Micah
(4: 1-3).   It is impossible to say with which of
these prophets it was original, or whether both
found it already at hand and used it.   In any case,
it is evidently a vision of eighth century origin.
" It may have been the ideal of the age."   (G. A.
Smith.)   Such a picture is marvelous coming from
any age prior to the actual advent of the Prince of
Peace.

3. The passage is Messianic.   The vision is of
Zion exalted and idealized.   All nations are seen
voluntarily streaming up to Jerusalem to be taught
Jehovah's law and to be instructed in his ways.
Zion becomes the religious metropolis of the world;
Jehovah, the umpire in all international disputes.
In the latter days, Isaiah predicts, an era of univer-
sal peace will be ushered in, and war shall be no
more.

4. Such a vision is of permanent value.   It was
not only the ideal of Isaiah's age, it is the goal also
of the gospel;   the only difference being that
through the Incarnate Word of Jehovah, Zion has
become spiritualized and decentralized, so that the

whole world, regardless of geography, shares in
the Messianic blessings of idyllic peace.

5. War is the arch-enemy of all social happiness.

Foreign Customs and Alliances (Chapter 2:5-22)

1. When Isaiah first beheld the vision of Jerusalem exalted as the Mecca of all nations in religion
and law (2: 2-4), he hoped to see his ideal realized
at once (v. 5); but the real Jerusalem of his day
fell too far below his ideal.

2. Before the prophet stood a crowd of soothsayers; yonder a company " filled with customs
from the east " (Babylonia); while the politicians
of Jerusalem were openly courting the friendship
and support of Assyria.

3. Accordingly, he breaks out in a vehement dia-
tribe against the nation's feverish lust for things
foreign: in particular their eagerness to trust to
foreign alliances in time of danger (v. 6). He also
denounces their wanton display of wealth and con-
fidence in their military resources (v. 7); and
their gross idolatry, which has permeated every
stratum of society beyond the possibility of forgiveness (vs. 8-11).

4. The prophet's chief point is, that Jerusalem's
best interests are being jeopardized through her
foolishly aping foreign customs, her worshiping
foreign gods, and her making alliances with foreign peoples, instead of relying on God.

5. For Jerusalem, therefore, he declares that a
day of reckoning is appointed (v. 12), when Jehovah will punish her proud and haughty inhabit-

ants (note the emphatic refrain repeated thrice in vs. 10, 19, 21). Then they will cast their idols to the moles and to the bats (v. 20).

6. The only real safety in all social crises is trust in God.

The Sins of the Aristocracy (Chapters 3-4)

1. The nation's chief sinners are those of the upper classes, the very ones to whom the people are looking for protection and guidance. Boldly and vehemently the prophet reproaches these (3: 1-4)—the army and its officers, the cabinet officials, judges and law givers, the professional prophets, and the diviners and skillful enchanters —because they have provoked by their unblushing wickedness the eyes of Jehovah's glory (3: 8, 9). That is to say, the soothsayers have sought to ascertain the will of deity and the magicians have sought to control that will, ignoring Jehovah.

2. All such dignitaries and so-called props of the commonwealth will be removed and a reign of terror will ensue. Society will be dissolved. In place of the elders and princes who now despoil the poor (3: 14), still more incompetent and capricious officers will rule, until anarchy destroys the state and Jerusalem is ruined and Judah is fallen (3: 8).

3. Isaiah also draws a picture of the women of Jerusalem (cf. Amos 4), painting them as "state dolls," who by their baneful influence on the government (3: 12) and their unbounded love of finery are undermining religion and morals in the home and poisoning the entire national life. He gives a catalogue of the twenty-one articles of their costly and curious attire (3: 18-23), and sternly

warns the proud ladies of Zion that all their gaudy paraphernalia will ere long be exchanged for captives' garb (3: 24—4: 1).

4. He further assures them that Jerusalem shall be cleansed of their social filth and that a mere remnant shall survive (4: 2-6), who, however, shall be the people's true glory in the eyes of the other nations (cf. 32: 15-18; 45: 8; 61: 10).

Judah's National Sins (Chapter 5)

1. The beautiful parable of the vineyard in 5: 1-7 stands closely related both to what precedes and to that which follows. Alas! when Jehovah looked that his vineyard should bring forth grapes, it brought forth wild grapes (v. 4); and when he "looked for justice (*mishpat*), behold oppression (*mispah*); and for righteousness (*sedakah*), behold a cry (*seakah*)". Isaiah frequently employs paranomasia, or play on words, as here in 5: 7.

2. He then names a few specimens of "wild grapes," or sins of the nations:

(1) Insatiable greed; but their crops will be only a tenth of the seed sown (vs. 8-10).

(2) Dissipation and disregard of the word and work of Jehovah; but carnival and carousing will end in captivity (vs. 11-17).

(3) Daring defiance of Jehovah, and willful contempt of the prophet's denunciations, boldly displayed by their challenging the "day of Jehovah" to come (vs. 18, 19).

(4) Hypocrisy and dissimulation, confusion of moral distinctions (v. 20).

(5) Political self-conceit, which scorns to submit to God's correction (v. 21).

(6) Misdirected power, heroic at wine drinking, but cowering before a bribe in avenging wrong (vs. 22-23).

3. Therefore, says the prophet, the worst is yet to come. Judah's national vitality is being sapped (v. 24), and a terrible invader (the Assyrian, as yet unnamed) is coming to smite them. It is Jehovah's judgment, and there will be no escape (vs. 25-30).

The Sins of the Masses (Chapter 6)

1. Chapter 6 contains an account of Isaiah's inaugural vision. It follows a discourse full of "woes," which, as we have seen, closes with a thunderstorm of doom unrelieved by any ray of hope (chapter 5).

2. One can easily fancy how the prophet, having spoken thus, would meet with counter opposition from his audience, and find it necessary to produce his credentials and demonstrate his authority for speaking in tones of such severity. No one, however, could give better proof of his commission than Isaiah. He had beheld a vision of Jehovah's holiness in contrast to his own unholiness; he had also received pardon, and been commissioned. From this point of view, chapter 6 becomes an apologetic. Embedded within it is the tacit claim of authority to pronounce "woes" upon others, because the prophet has already pronounced "woe" upon himself. This best accounts for the editorial insertion of this vision at this point among Isaiah's prophecies. " Unclean lips " was the nation's chief sin (6: 5).

3. But Isaiah's commission was a hard one. We must not suppose that the prophet, from his subsequent experience, read into his original commission elements which it did not convey to his mind at the time; for, as Skinner wisely observes, " by doing so we mistake the prophet's attitude to his

work." From the very first Isaiah labored under the depressing conviction that he would only harden the people in unbelief (6: 9-13).

4. This was as obvious as it was inevitable. Sin, like water, percolates most rapidly downward. The upper classes were already callous in unbelief; it was, therefore, only a matter of time when the masses also should become insensible to spiritual things: their hearts fat, their ears heavy, and their eyes smeared.

Summary of Isaiah's Social Discourses

1. All social evils are traceable ultimately to a want of true religion: apathy towards, and rebellion against God. Formal religion is but a common species of hypocrisy (chapter 1).

2. Social happiness is rendered impossible by war; therefore, to have satisfactory social conditions there must be peace (2: 1-4).

3. Foreign alliances, soothsaying and idolatry are all proofs of distrust in God. " Blessed is the nation whose God is Jehovah " (2: 5-22).

4. Woe to the nation whose political and religious leaders are corrupt. The next step is anarchy, and after that, exile. Double woe when the leading women of a community think only of fashion and of self, of bracelets and head-tires, festival robes and mantles, shawls and veils; ruin then is dangerously near (3-4).

5. Judah's national sins were outstanding, namely, oppression and wrong-doing (5: 7), inordinate greed (5: 8), careless high-living (5: 11), blatant unbelief in a divine Providence (5: 18), willful self-deception (5: 20), unwillingness to be

criticised (5: 21), bribery or " graft " (5: 22, 23). Such a nation of sinners was ill prepared to resist a foreign foe (5: 24-30).

6. The sins of the aristocracy filter downward; as patricians, so plebeians. Judah's condition was well-nigh hopeless. The whole nation was becoming spiritually insensible. They had eyes but they could not see. Only judgment could avail—" the righteous judgment of the forgotten God." A " holy seed," however, still existed in Israel's stock (6: 13).

THEREFORE THE LORD HIMSELF WILL GIVE YOU A SIGN: BEHOLD A VIRGIN SHALL CONCEIVE, AND BEAR A SON, AND SHALL CALL HIS NAME IMMANUEL.

ISA. 7: 14.

FOR UNTO US A CHILD IS BORN, UNTO US A SON IS GIVEN; AND THE GOVERNMENT SHALL BE UPON HIS SHOULDER: AND HIS NAME SHALL BE CALLED WONDERFUL, COUNSELLOR, MIGHTY GOD, EVERLASTING FATHER, PRINCE OF PEACE.

ISA. 9: 6.

THEREFORE WITH JOY SHALL YE DRAW WATER OUT OF THE WELLS OF SALVATION.

ISA. 12: 3.

STUDY SEVEN

JUDAH'S POLITICAL ENTANGLEMENTS
(CHAPTERS 7-12)

The Syro-Ephraimitic Uprising (Chapter 7:1-9)

1. The so-called Syro-Ephraimitic war of 734 B. C. is one of the very great crises in Isaiah's ministry. Side by side there stood the young prophet of perhaps thirty years, and the still younger king of not more than twenty-one, with policies diametrically opposed. Pekah of North Israel and Rezin of Damascus, in attempting to defend themselves against the Assyrians, coveted an ally in the king of Jerusalem. But Ahaz preferred the friendship of Assyria, and refused to enter into alliance with them; as Jotham seems to have done before him (2 Kings 15: 37).

2. Accordingly Pekah and Rezin combined to dethrone Ahaz and to put in his place one who would ally with them (Isa. 7: 6). But when news came of their threatened attack Ahaz was panic-stricken and all Jerusalem with him (7: 2). He resolved to apply at once to Assyria for assistance, sending ambassadors with many precious treasures, both royal and sacred (2 Kings 16: 7, 8).

3. At this juncture Isaiah is bidden by Jehovah to take his son, Shear-jashub, and go forth to meet King Ahaz, who is busy preparing for siege, repairing the fortifications and in particular securing the city's water supply. The prophet obeys, and expostulates with Ahaz concerning the fatal step he is about to take by calling in the aid of Assyria,

and assures him that the two petty kingdoms of
North Israel and Syria are but " two tails of smok-
ing firebrands " (7: 3, 4). On the one side, it is
only Rezin with Damascus, and the mere son of
Remaliah with Samaria; whereas, on the other
side is Jehovah with Jerusalem (7: 8, 9).

4. Here for the first time, Isaiah appears in the
rôle of a practical statesman; a position which he
continues to occupy all his life, and the duties of
which he more and more influentially discharges.

Ahaz, the King of No-Faith (Chapter 7: 10-25)

1. Isaiah in his interview with Ahaz emphasized
faith; to the prophet faith meant security and
quietness (7: 4, 9). Isaiah saw clearly that the
only path of safety was loyalty to Jehovah, and in-
dependence of foreign alliances. Hosea had previ-
ously advocated the same policy to North Israel
(Hosea 14: 2, 3).

2. But Ahaz did not possess this faculty of
mind; wherefore, Jehovah graciously offers him a
sign in order to make faith easy as possible. The
king may choose either earthquake or lightning
(7: 11). Ahaz refuses both, in order afterwards
not to be bound by God's word. He has a secret
dread of the truth. Accordingly Jehovah unasked
determines to give him a sign, a child, Immanuel,
" God with us " (7: 14), the stages of whose life
will reveal the rapid changes which will take place
in the land of Judah in the near future.

3. The passage is implicitly Messianic. The un-
derlying truth of the prophecy is the necessity of
faith in Jehovah's power to save. Because of the

king's unbelief, Judah is to become the theatre of war between Assyria and Egypt (7: 18, 19). The country will be left ravaged, depopulated and uncultivated, and become the hunting ground of nomads (7: 21-25), all because of the short-sighted policy of Ahaz, the king of No-Faith.

No Conspiracy Successful without God
(Chapters 8:1 — 9:7)

1. By means of a great tablet, posted in a conspicuous place, bearing the motto Maher-shalal-hash-baz, "hasting to the spoil, hurrying to the prey," Isaiah announced publicly the issue of Assyria's attack on Damascus (732 B. C.). Isaiah also appropriated the motto as a living sign, naming his newborn son Maher-shalal-hash-baz (8: 1-4).

2. Judah he predicts will barely escape; for she has despised the softly flowing waters of Shiloh— the symbol of Jehovah's silent power and gracious rule—for the waters of the river Euphrates—the power of Assyria (8: 5-8).

3. Yet "God is with us," proclaims the prophet, and conspiracy is impossible unless God too is against us. With God on our side as a sanctuary, there is no reason for fear; the only possible conspiracy is when Jehovah fights against us on the side of the enemy (8: 9-15).

4. However, the prophet's message of promise and salvation finds no welcome. It must therefore remain bound up and sealed, i. e., committed to Isaiah's disciples for future use (8: 16-18). Nevertheless out of the coming darkness will flash forth eventually a great light: " For unto us a child is born, unto us a son is given." In his day, the empire of David will be established upon a

basis of justice and righteousness (8: 19—9: 7).
The Messianic scion is the ground of the prophet's
hope; which hope, though unappreciated, he thus
early in his ministry commits, written and sealed,
to his inner circle of " disciples."

Accumulated Wrath (Chapters 9:8 — 10:4)

1. In an artistic poem composed of four strophes,
the prophet describes the great calamities which
Jehovah has sent upon North Israel to warn them
of their wickedness. Each strophe closes with an
awful but most effective refrain, " for all this his
anger is not turned away, but his hand is stretched
out still " (9: 12, 17, 21; 10: 4; cf. 5: 25).

2. But Jehovah's judgments have gone unheeded, although North Israel has already suffered untold misfortunes (cf. Amos 4: 6-11). Isaiah spec-
ifies some of them and foretells others yet to come:

(1) Foreign invasion; but loss of territory made
no lasting impression upon their arrogant and
stubborn hearts (9: 8-12).

(2) Defeat in battle; but even the loss of their
young men and the cries of their suffering widows
and orphans did not bring them to repentance (9:
13-17).

(3) Anarchy; but even internecine strife, rag-
ing like a blazing forest fire, was not sufficient to
cause them to take heed (9: 18-21).

(4) Now captivity stares them in the face; yet
with the day of visitation confronting them, and
with the prospect of condemnation from the Supreme Judge, and with no possibility of escape,
they still persist in their downward course (10:
1-4).

3. "For all this his anger is not turned away, but his hand is stretched out still." Divine discipline has failed; only judgment remains.

Assyria, an Instrument of Jehovah
(Chapter 10:5-34)

1. Chapter 10: 5-34 dates also from the reign of Ahaz. Verse 20 is decidedly in favor of this view; verses 28-32 do not describe Sennacherib's route of invasion in 701 B. C., but rather that of the great Assyrian conqueror, as, *in Isaiah's mind*, he would naturally plan it after taking Samaria. Moreover, the tone of verses 12, 21-23 shows that the Assyrians' devastation of the land is not yet complete; while 2 Chron. 28: 20, 21 describes the exact conditions which the prophecy demands as an appropriate historic setting, namely, that instead of Judah receiving help from the Assyrians, the Assyrians treated the Judeans as enemies, and exacted heavy tribute.

2. The prophet's main point is that the great Assyrian despot is but the unconcious rod of Jehovah's anger, a mere instrument in God's hands, with which he is going to punish his people. In his carnal self-confidence and barbarous lust of plunder and conquest, the Assyrian may boast of his achievements, but he is really nothing more than an axe or a saw in the hands of the divine Woodsman, who will lay him low so soon as he has accomplished his purpose (10: 5-19; cf. "Cyrus," 45: 4).

3. Only a remnant, however, shall be saved (10: 20-23). They will return to their land "after the manner of Egypt" (10: 24-27); for the prophet here is not speaking of the people's conversion to Jehovah, as some think, but of their return from exile. Therefore let not Judah fear, for Jehovah is

a God of righteousness, and eventually he will demonstrate also that he is greater than the gods of the Assyrians, who seem at the present to be supreme (10: 28-34).

Israel's Return from Exile (Chapters 11-12)

1. Isaiah's vision of Israel's future reached beyond the exile, which was steadily taking place before his eyes, to Israel's return. A prediction to the same effect had already been made by Amos (9: 14, 15). The downfall of Assyria is the signal for the commencement of a new era in Israel's history.

2. Assyria has no future, her downfall is fatal; Judah has a future, her calamities are only disciplinary. The house of Jesse has not wholly lost its recuperative power. An Ideal Prince will be raised up, in whose advent all nature will rejoice, even dumb animals (11: 1-9).

3. Him also the nations will seek (11: 10). The prophet had predicted this essentially before (2: 2-4).

4. In his days, righteousness and wisdom will be diffused; "For the earth shall be full of the knowledge of Jehovah, as the waters cover the sea" (11: 9).

5. A second great exodus will take place, for the Lord shall set his hand again " the second time " to recover the remnant of his people " from the four corners of the earth " (11: 11, 12). In that day, " Ephraim shall not envy Judah and Judah shall not vex Ephraim " (11: 13).

6. Then the reunited nation, redeemed and occupying their rightful territory (11: 14-16), shall sing a hymn of thanksgiving (12: 1-6), as ancient Israel did after their exodus from Egypt (cf. Exod. 15); and they shall further proclaim the salvation of Jehovah to all the earth (12: 5).

Summary of Isaiah's Political Discourses
(734-732 B.C.)

1. " Take heed and be quiet; fear not, neither let thy heart be faint;" " If ye will not believe, surely ye shall not be established " (7 : 4, 9). This was the essence of Isaiah's advice to Ahaz when threatened by the two kingdoms from the north— Ephraim and Syria.

2. "For before the child (Immanuel) shall know to refuse the evil and choose the good, the land whose two kings thou abhorrest shall be forsaken" (7: 16); and so it was. Within two years both Pekah and Rezin were dethroned and their richest spoils taken away to Assyria (732 B. C.).

3. " Say ye not, A conspiracy, concerning all whereof this people shall say, A conspiracy: neither fear ye their fear, nor be in dread thereof. Jehovah of hosts, him shall ye sanctify; and let him be your fear, and let him be your dread " (8 : 12, 13).

4. " The Lord sent a word into Jacob, and it hath lighted upon Israel " (9: 8); judgment upon judgment, and calamity upon calamity, but Jehovah's warnings had notwithstanding all passed unheeded. "For all this his anger is not turned away, but his hand is stretched out still " (9: 12, 17, 21; 10: 4).

5. " O my people, that dwellest in Zion, be not afraid of the Assyrians: though he smite thee with the rod, and lift up his staff against thee, after the manner of Egypt. For yet a very little while, and the indignation against thee shall be accomplished, and mine anger shall be directed to his destruction " (10: 24, 25). Which means that if the Assyrian bondage is to be like the Egyptian, there will be a correspondingly glorious deliverance.

6. Finally, a Messiah-Branch will grow out of

the root of Jesse, bringing salvation and peace not only to the returned exiles, but also to the nations (11: 10). Then shall the redeemed with joy draw water out of the wells of salvation, and proclaim their salvation to the end of the earth (12: 3, 5).

ONE CALLETH UNTO ME OUT OF SEIR, WATCHMAN, WHAT OF THE NIGHT? WATCHMAN, WHAT OF THE NIGHT? THE WATCHMAN SAID, THE MORNING COMETH, AND ALSO THE NIGHT: IF YE WILL INQUIRE, INQUIRE YE: TURN YE, COME.

ISA. 21: 11, 12.

STUDY EIGHT

ISAIAH'S "BURDENS" CONCERNING FOREIGN
NATIONS (CHAPTERS 13-23, 34-35)

Concerning Babylon
(Chapters 13:1 — 14:23; 21:1-10)

1. Isaiah's horizon was world-wide. He was a
close observer of national movements, and passed
in review the foreign nations whose destinies affected Judah, as did Amos (chapters 1-2), Jeremiah (chapters 46-51), and Ezekiel (chapters
25-32).

2. First among his foreign prophecies stands the
oracle concerning Babylon (13: 1—14: 23), in
which he predicts the utter destruction of the city
(13: 2-22) and sings a dirge or taunt-song over her
fallen king (14: 4-23). The king alluded to, however, is almost beyond doubt an Assyrian not a
Babylonian monarch of the eighth century (so
Winckler, Cheyne, Cobb and others); the brief
prophecy immediately following in 14: 24-27 concerning " Assyria " confirms this interpretation.
Moreover it was subsequent to this that Sennacherib made Nineveh the capital and removed the
seat of his empire thither.

3. The other brief oracle concerning Babylon
(21: 1-10) describes the city's fall as imminent.
Both oracles stand or fall together as genuine
prophecies of Isaiah. Both seem to have been
written in Jerusalem (13: 2; 21: 9-10). It cannot
be said that either is absolutely unrelated in
thought and language to Isaiah's age (14: 13; 21:
2); each foretells the doom to fall on Babylon
(13: 19; 21: 9), at the hands of the Medes (13: 17;
21: 2); and each describes the Israelites as already
in exile—but not necessarily *all* Israel. The best
historical setting for 13: 1—14: 23, therefore,
seems to be the period between 732-722 B. C.; and
for 21: 1-10, 709 B. C. A perfectly satisfactory

historical background, however, should not be expected for an oracle dealing with " the day of Jehovah " (13: 6, 9).

4. It is enough that the two great lessons of the redemption and comfort of Israel are taught by these oracles (14: 1-2; 21: 9-10), and that the prophet announces Babylon's impending doom with feelings of sincere emotion (21: 3).

Concerning Moab (Chapters 15-16)

1. This ancient oracle against Moab, whose dirge-like meter resembles that of chapters 13-14, is composed of two separate prophecies belonging to two different periods in Isaiah's ministry (16: 13).

2. Chapters 15: 1—16: 12 describe Moab's woeful condition in 734 B. C., just after Tiglath-pileser, king of Assyria, had overrun Galilee and the region east of the Jordan, probably threatening Moab (2 Kings 15: 29). Chapter 16: 13-14 is a brief epilogue to the former prophecy, predicting the actual capture of Moab " within three years " (711 B. C.).

3. The principal points of interest in the oracle are:

(1) The prophet's tender sympathy for Moab in her affliction (15: 5; 16: 11). Isaiah mingles his own tears with those of the Moabites. " There is no prophecy in the book of Isaiah in which the heart of the prophet is so painfully moved by what his spirit beholds and his mouth must prophesy." (Delitzsch.)

(2) Moab's pathetic appeal for shelter from her foes; particularly the ground on which she urges it, namely, the Messianic hope that the Davidic dynasty shall always stand and be able to repulse its foes (16: 5). The passage is an echo of 9: 5-7.

(3) The promise that a remnant of Moab, though small, shall be saved (16: 14). Wearied of prayer to Chemosh in his high places, the prophet predicts that Moab will seek the living God (16: 12).

Concerning Philistia and Damascus
(Chapters 14:28-32; 17:1-14)

1. The oracle concerning Philistia (14: 28-32) is dated, "in the year that king Ahaz died" (727 B. C.). Tiglath-pileser III., king of Assyria, died in the same year.

2. In the first half of the oracle (vs. 29-30), the Philistines are bidden not to rejoice over the death of the great Assyrian "serpent" (Tiglath-pileser III.), as he will be succeeded by an "adder" (Shalmaneser IV.), and he in turn by a "fiery flying serpent" (Sargon II.), each one more destructive than his predecessor.

3. In the second half (vs. 31-32), Isaiah warns the Philistines of the Assyrians' approach, and of Jerusalem's unwillingness to form an alliance with them, because faith in Jehovah renders Jerusalem inviolable; therefore, Philistia's messengers may as well return home, for everything human is going down.

4. In the oracle concerning Damascus, which also includes North Israel in its scope (17: 1-14), Isaiah predicts the fate of the two allies—Syria and Ephraim— in the Syro-Ephraimitic war (734 B. C.), with a promise that only a scanty remnant will survive (17: 6).

5. The cause of Israel's sad desolation, the prophet boldly declares, is their forgetfulness of God (17: 10); on the other hand, their unnamed foes (the Assyrians, undoubtedly) will themselves

be vanquished between evening and daybreak
(17: 14).

Concerning Egypt and Ethiopia (Chapters 18-20)

1. Three distinct prophecies are addressed to
Egypt and Ethiopia. Both these lands in Isaiah's
period were ruled over by a single king from
Napata in Ethiopia.

2. The first (chapter 18) describes Ethiopia as
in great excitement, sending ambassadors hither
and thither—possibly all the way to Jerusalem—
ostensibly seeking aid in making preparations for
war. Assyria had already taken Damascus (732
B. C.) and Samaria (722 B. C.); consequently,
Egypt and Ethiopia were in great fear of invasion.
Isaiah bids the ambassadors to return home and
quietly watch Jehovah thwart Assyria's self-confi-
dent attempt to subjugate Judah; and he adds that
when the Ethiopians have seen God's hand in the
coming deliverance of Judah and Jerusalem (701
B. C.) and Samaria (722 B. C.); consequently,
abode in Mount Zion (cf. 2 Chron. 32: 23; Ps. 68:
31; Isa. 45: 14).

3. The second oracle (chapter 19) contains both
a threat (vs. 1-17) and a promise (vs. 18-25), and
is one of Isaiah's most remarkable foreign prophecies (720 B. C.). Egypt is smitten and thereby
led to abandon her idols for the worship of Jehovah (vs. 19-22). More remarkable still, it is prophesied that " in that day " Egypt and Assyria will
join with Judah in a triple alliance of common
worship to Jehovah and of blessing to others (vs.
23-25). The prophecy is a marvelous " missionary
sermon," worthy of a place alongside Paul's sermon on Mars' Hill.

4. The third prophecy (chapter 20) is a brief
symbolic prediction of Assyria's victory over Egypt

and Ethiopia in 711 B. C. By donning a captive's garb for three years, Isaiah attempts to teach the citizens of Jerusalem that the siege of Ashdod (v. 1) was but a means to an end in Sargon's plan of campaign, and that it was sheer folly for the Egyptian party in Jerusalem, who were ever urging reliance upon Egypt, to look in that direction for help. In this graphic manner Isaiah symbolized the shameful fate which later befell the Egyptians at the hands of Sargon (cf. Mic. 1: 8).

Concerning Edom and Arabia
(Chapters 21:11-17; 34-35; 63:1-6)

1. Of the three brief oracles concerning Edom in the book of Isaiah, that in 21: 11-12 is " the only gentle utterance in the Old Testament upon Israel's hereditary foe." In it the prophet, in vision, beholds Edom in great anxiety sending messengers to inquire how far gone is their night of darkness and distress. The prophet's answer is disappointing, though its tone is sympathetic. The outlook is chequered. Dawn struggles with darkness. But if the messengers will come again, there may be additional tidings later (711 B. C.).

2. A second prophecy against " all the nations," but against Edom in particular, is the fierce cry for justice in chapter 34 (701 B. C.). Its tone is the tone of judgment. Edom is guilty of high crimes against Zion (34: 8), therefore she is doomed to destruction. On the other hand, Israel's scattered ones shall return from exile and " obtain gladness and joy, and sorrow and sighing shall flee away " (chapter 35).

3. Shortly after this, Isaiah lifts his eye again and beholds a solitary majestic warrior coming from the direction of Edom, in clothing besprinkled with blood, and learns on inquiry that a terrible judgment of the nations has taken place

on the soil of Edom (63: 1-6). The prophecy is a
drama of divine vengeance on those who rejoiced
in Judah's devastation and Jerusalem's humiliation in 701 B. C. This picture of Jehovah graph-
ically prefigures the agony and passion of the Saviour who also " trod the winepress alone."

4. The brief oracle concerning Arabia in 21: 13-
17 is a sympathetic appeal to the Temanites to
give bread and water to the caravans of Dedan,
who have been driven by war from their usual
route of travel. For, says the prophet, " within a
year " their fate will have been sealed and only a
small remnant will survive (711 B. C.).

Concerning the Foreign Temper within the Theocracy (Chapter 22)

1. Isaiah pauses, as it were, in his series of
warnings to foreign nations to rebuke the foreign
temper of the frivolous inhabitants of Jerusalem,
and in particular Shebna, a high official in the government (chapter 22). The minatory tone of the
oracle points to the year 711 B. C., when Sargon
invaded Judah, rather than to a temporary raising
of the blockade of Jerusalem by Sennacherib in
701 B. C.

2. In verses 1-14 the prophet draws a picture of
the reckless and God-ignoring citizens of the capital, who venture to indulge themselves in hilarious
eating and drinking, when the enemy at that very
moment is standing before the gates of the city.
Very differently the impending catastrophe affects
Isaiah, who weeps bitterly and refuses to be comforted because of the destruction of his people.
With prophetic courage he declares that such godless impenitence and spiritual insensibility are sins
beyond the possibility of forgiveness (v. 14).

3. In verses 15-25 Isaiah directs a personal message—the only philippic in his book—to Shebna,

the comptroller of the palace, in which he predicts his deposition from office and degradation to a lower and less honorable position in the royal service.

4. Shebna seems to have been an ostentatious foreigner, perhaps a Syrian by birth, quite possibly one of the Egyptian party, whose policy was antagonistic to that of Isaiah and the king. On the other hand, Eliakim, who was appointed in his place, probably represented the true policy of the state; yet he also seems eventually to have forfeited his position of trust through nepotism— showing unwarrantable favors to his relatives. Isaiah's prediction of Shebna's fall was evidently fulfilled (36: 3; 37: 2).

Concerning Tyre (Chapter 23). Summary

1. In this last of Isaiah's foreign oracles (chapter 23), the prophet predicts that Tyre shall be laid waste (v. 1), her commercial glory humbled (v. 9), her colonies become independent of her (v. 10), and she herself forgotten for " seventy years " (v. 15); but, "after the end of seventy years," her trade will revive, her business prosperity will return, and she will dedicate her gains in merchandise as holy to Jehovah (v. 18). The best date for this oracle is shortly before 722 B. C.

2. In summing up the lessons of permanent value taught by these foreign oracles, emphasis should be laid on the following points:

(1) That Babylon falls because of arrogancy and pride, whereas Israel is redeemed through Jehovah's gracious compassion (13: 11; 14: 1-2).

(2) That Moab bases her appeal to Zion for shelter on the permanent character of the Davidic dynasty, as expressed in the Messianic hope cur-

rent in Israel, namely, that " a throne shall be established in loving kindness " (16: 4-5).

(3) That the Philistines are not allowed to ally themselves with Judah against Assyria, because Jerusalem is already inviolable through faith in Jehovah (14: 32), and that the allied forces of Damascus and Israel had failed in the Syro-Ephraimitic war because they forsook the God of their salvation for idols (17: 10).

(4) That Ethiopia is converted to Jehovah through seeing God's hand in history (18: 7), and that Egypt is won to Jehovah's worship through divine discipline (19: 22).

(5) That Edom's fickle cry for light in the night (21: 11-12) is not deep or sincere enough to secure her from rejoicing over Judah's calamities, and therefore not sufficient to avert her deserved doom (34: 10).

(6) That careless, godless abandon on the part of people in imminent peril of siege is an unpardonable sin and foreign to the spirit of the theocracy (22: 14); and that a man's pride, even of one who is a high officer of state, " shall bring him low " (22: 16, 19).

(7) And lastly, that the profits derived from merchandise are no better morally than the hire of a harlot unless consecrated to the service of Jehovah (23: 18). In short, that the heathen, as well as Israel, are responsible to God, and may share if they wish in his mercy and grace.

AND IN THIS MOUNTAIN WILL JEHOVAH OF HOSTS MAKE UNTO ALL PEOPLES A FEAST OF FAT THINGS, A FEAST OF WINES ON THE LEES, OF FAT THINGS FULL OF MARROW, OF WINES ON THE LEES WELL REFINED.

ISA. 25: 6.

HE HATH SWALLOWED UP DEATH FOR EVER; AND THE LORD JEHOVAH WILL WIPE AWAY TEARS FROM OFF ALL FACES; AND THE REPROACH OF HIS PEOPLE WILL HE TAKE AWAY FROM OFF ALL THE EARTH; FOR JEHOVAH HATH SPOKEN IT.

ISA. 25: 8.

THOU WILT KEEP HIM IN PERFECT PEACE, WHOSE MIND IS STAYED ON THEE; BECAUSE HE TRUSTETH IN THEE.

ISA. 26: 3.

THY DEAD SHALL LIVE; MY DEAD BODIES SHALL ARISE. AWAKE AND SING, YE THAT DWELL IN THE DUST; FOR THY DEW IS AS THE DEW OF HERBS, AND THE EARTH SHALL CAST FORTH THE DEAD.

ISA. 26: 19.

STUDY NINE

SPIRITUAL MESSAGES OF SALVATION
(CHAPTERS 24-27)

Prophecy or Apocalypse?

1. It is difficult to distinguish between prophecy and apocalypse. Prophecy, however, usually foretells a definite future which has its foundations in the present; apocalypse directs the mind more abstractly to the future in contrast with the present.

2. Strictly speaking chapters 24-27 are prophecy, not apocalypse. No one ascends into heaven or talks with an angel, as in Dan. 7 and Rev. 4. They can, therefore, be considered apocalypse only in the sense that certain things are predicted as sure to come to pass.

3. Isaiah was fond of this kind of prophecy. He frequently lifts his reader out of the sphere of mere history to paint pictures of the far-off distant future (2: 2-4; 4: 2-6; 11: 6-16; 30: 27-33). In chapters 24-27 we are especially impressed by the scope of his imagination.

4. These prophecies stand closely related to chapters 13-23. They express the same tender emotion as that already observed in 21: 3, 10; 15: 5; 16: 11, and sum up as in one grand finale the prophet's oracles to Israel's neighbors. For religious importance they stand second to none in the book of Isaiah, teaching the necessity of divine discipline and the glorious redemption awaiting the faithful in Israel.

5. They are a spiritual commentary on the great Assyrian crisis of the eighth century, and seem to have sprung from the period prior to the fall of Samaria (722 B. C.), or possibly just before the invasion of Sennacherib in 701 B. C. They are mes-

sages intended not for declamation but for meditation, and were probably addressed more particularly to the prophet's inner circle of "disciples" (8: 16).

Waves of Approaching Judgment (Chapter 24)

1. A general judgment is on the way (v. 1), which will level all classes of society (v. 2), " because they have transgressed the laws, violated the statutes, broken the everlasting covenant " (v. 5). Even "the earth " (in particular Judah) becomes polluted by Israel's sins and shares their guilt. Nature is frequently described in the Old Testament as sympathetic. " Man not only governs nature, he infects her." (G. A. Smith.)

2. Few mortals remain (v. 6), the merry-hearted sigh (v. 7), the harp is silent (v. 8), Judah's cities (the word "city" in verses 10, 12 is collective) are broken down, and mirth has vanished (v. 11); only a sorry remnant is left of all the nations east and west to glorify the majesty of Jehovah (vs. 13-15).

3. The prophet fancies he hears songs of deliverance, but alas! they are premature; more judgment must follow (v. 16). Universal catastrophe is about to burst in on every side like a terrible flood (v. 18). Neither the greatest of earth's kings nor even the guardian princes of heaven will escape (v. 21). Indeed, the sun and moon will lose their brightness, in token that God is angry with the world; for Jehovah will reign as sovereign over Zion in glory (v. 23).

4. Thus beyond the coming waves of judgment there lies a glorious salvation; Zion's enemies will be punished, while Zion herself shall emerge triumphant.

Songs of the Redeemed (Chapter 25)

1. In chapter 25 the prophet transports himself to the period after the Assyrian catastrophe and, identifying himself with the redeemed, puts into their mouths songs of praise and thanksgiving for their deliverance. His aim is not political but religious.

2. Verses 1-5 are a hymn of thanksgiving to Jehovah for deliverance from the Assyrians, and also a confession of faith on the part of heathen cities ("city" is here again collective as in 24: 10, 12), whose surviving remnants now recognize the wonderful might of Jehovah.

3. Verses 6-8 describe Jehovah's bountiful banquet on Mount Zion to all nations, who, in keeping with 2: 2-4, come up to Jerusalem to celebrate "a feast of fat things," rich and marrowy. While the people are present at the banquet, Jehovah graciously removes their spiritual blindness so that they behold him as the true dispenser of life and grace. He also abolishes violent death, that is to say, war (cf. 2: 4), and its sad accompaniment, "tears"; so that "the earth" (Judah in particular) is no longer the battlefield of the nations, but the blessed abode of the redeemed, living in peace and happiness.

4. Verses 9-12 unfold in hymn-like language how in that day Jehovah's people will rejoice that in the midst of desolating calamities which are safely past, they waited patiently for Jehovah's salvation and, in consequence, now enjoy peace and rest; whereas Moab and all other enemies of Israel are described as suffering untold anguish and desolation.

5. The chapter is "an enhanced echo of the song on the seashore in Exodus 15." (Orelli.)

Life from the Dead (Chapter 26:1-19)

1. In chapter 26: 1-19 Judah sings a song over Jerusalem, the impregnable city of God. The prophet, taking again his stand with the redeemed remnant of the nation, vividly portrays their thankful trust in Jehovah, who has been unto them a veritable " Rock of ages " (v. 4).

2. Jerusalem was impregnable because surrounded by the walls of Jehovah's salvation (v. 1); yet she is ever accessible to all who keep faith (v. 2), and the secure abode of all those whose dispositions are firmly stayed on Jehovah (v. 3). Other cities ("city" in verse 5 is without the article and therefore collective) have been brought low, but in Jerusalem, the impregnable city of Jehovah, there is safety.

3. Looking back over their past experiences the redeemed community at length recognize that by patiently waiting on God to come to judgment they were taught righteousness (vs. 8, 9); the wicked, on the contrary, who are incapable of learning righteousness, will be judged (v. 10).

4. At this point the prophet pauses to reflect on the destruction of the nation's adversaries (v. 11), and on the people's peaceful condition as the result of Jehovah's deliverance of them from foreign oppressors who are now dead and forgotten (vs. 12-14). He also recalls how Jehovah increased the nation (v. 15), how they prayed to him in their distress (v. 16), and how they utterly failed in attempting to save themselves (vs. 17-18).

5. With hope, therefore, he exclaims, Let Jehovah's dead ones live! Let Israel's dead bodies arise! Jehovah will bring life from the dead! (v. 19.) This is the first clear statement of the resurrection in the Old Testament. But it is national

and restricted to Israel even here (cf. v. 14), and is merely Isaiah's method of expressing a hope of the return of Israel's faithful ones from captivity (cf. Hos. 6: 2; Ezek. 37: 1-14; Dan. 12: 2).

Israel's Chastisements Salutary
(Chapters 36:20 — 27:13)

1. In chapter 26: 20, 21 the prophet exhorts his own people, his disciples, to continue a little longer in the solitude of prayer, till God's wrath is overpast. They are to be saved, but the land as a whole is incapable of salvation. Yet in that day (27: 1) the agents of destruction shall themselves be destroyed: viz., " the swift serpent," Assyria; " the crooked serpent," Babylonia; and the sea " monster," Egypt.

2. The true vineyard of Jehovah, which these three great heathen world-powers have like ravenous beasts laid waste, will henceforth be safely guarded against the briars and thorns of foreign invasion (27: 2-4; cf. 5: 1-7); and it will flourish so gloriously that the whole earth shall be filled with its fruit (27: 6; cf. 4: 2). The language here is that of prophecy, not apocalypse (cf. 37: 31).

3. Notwithstanding all, Jehovah's chastisements of Israel were light compared with the judgments of Jehovah upon other nations (27: 7, 8). Theirs were punitive; Israel's, remedial. Israel he sifted; the nations he destroyed. In their case his object was annihilation: in Israel's, salvation. Forgiveness, therefore, is ever possible, if "Jacob" will only renounce his sins and forsake his idolatry (27: 9).

4. But Judah, like Ephraim in Hosea's time (Hos. 4: 17), is wedded to her idols, hence her fortified cities ("city" in 27: 10 is collective, as in 24: 10-12; 25: 2; 26: 5) will become solitary and for-

saken (27: 10-11). When, however, Israel repents, Jehovah will spare no pains to gather "one by one" the remnant of his people from Assyria and Egypt (cf. 11: 11); and together they shall once more worship Jehovah in the holy mountain at Jerusalem (27: 12-13).

The Historical Standpoint of the Author

1. The prophet's fundamental standpoint in chapters 24-27 is the same as that of the author of 2: 2-4 and chapters 13-23, namely, that of the eighth century B. C. As to his style and figures also, "everything is Isaianic," and "has an Isaianic ring." (Delitzsch.)

2. Yet the prophet not infrequently throws himself forward into the remote future, oscillating backwards and forwards between his own times and those of Israel's restoration. It is especially noteworthy how he sustains himself in a long and continued transportation of himself to the period of Israel's redemption. He even studies to identify himself with the new Israel which will emerge out of the present chaos of political events. His visions of Israel's redemption carry him in ecstasy far away into the remote future, to a time when the nation's sufferings are all over; so that when he writes down what he saw in vision he describes it as a discipline that is past.

3. For example, in 25: 1-8 the prophet, transported to the end of time, celebrates what he saw in song, and describes how the fall of the world-empire is followed by the conversion of the heathen. In 26: 8-9 he looks back into the past from the standpoint of the redeemed in the last days, and tells how Israel longingly waited for the manifestation of God's righteousness which has now taken place. While in 27: 7-9, he places himself

in the midst of the nation's sufferings, in full view of their glorious future, and portrays how Jehovah's dealings with Israel have not been the punishment of wrath, but the discipline of love.

4. This kind of apocalypse, indeed, was to be expected from the very beginning of this group of prophecies, which are introduced with the word, " Behold!" Such a manner of introduction is peculiar to Isaiah, and of itself leads us to expect a message which is unique.

The Value of Chapters 24-27 to Isaiah's Age

1. The practical religious value of these prophecies to Isaiah's own age would be very great. They would bring untold spiritual comfort to the theocracy.

2. In a period of war and repeated foreign invasion (734-722 B. C.), when but few men were left in the land (24: 6, 13; 26: 18) and Judah's cities were laid waste and desolate (24: 10, 12; 25: 2; 26: 5; 27: 10) and music and gladness were wanting (24: 8), when the nation still clung to their idols (27: 9) and the Assyrians' work of destruction was still incomplete, other calamities being sure to follow (24: 16); it would certainly be comforting to know that forgiveness was still possible (27: 9), that Jehovah was still the keeper of his vineyard (27: 3-4), that his judgments were to last but for a little moment (26: 20), and that though his people should be scattered, he would soon carefully gather them " one by one " (27: 12-13), and that in company with other nations they would feast together on Mount Zion as Jehovah's guests (25: 6, 7, 10). On the other hand, the prophet assures his hearers that their enemies, Moab (25: 10), Assyria, Babylon and Egypt (27: 1) shall be trodden down and destroyed and that Jerusalem

shall henceforth become the center of life and religion to all nations (24: 23; 25: 6; 27: 13).

3. Such faith in Jehovah, such exhortations, and such songs and confessions of the redeemed, seen in vision, would be a source of rich spiritual comfort to the few suffering saints in Judah and Jerusalem, and a guiding star to the faithful disciples of the prophet's inner circle; and through them a ground of hope to the generations to come, upon whom similar judgments would inevitably descend.

4. As a matter of fact, it is pretty generally recognized even by the most radical critics that these prophecies have at least an Isaianic basis.

For It is Precept upon Precept, Precept upon Precept; Line upon Line, Line upon Line; Here a Little, There a Little.

Isa. 28: 10.

Therefore Thus Saith the Lord Jehovah, Behold I Lay in Zion for a Foundation a Stone, a Tried Stone, a Precious Corner Stone of sure Foundation: He that Believeth Shall not be in Haste.

Isa. 28: 16.

For the Bed is Shorter than that a Man can Stretch Himself on It; and the Covering Narrower than that He can Wrap Himself in It.

Isa. 28: 20.

And a Man Shall be as a Hiding-place from the Wind, and a Covert from the Tempest, as Streams of Water in a Dry Place, as the Shade of a Great Rock in a Weary Land.

Isa. 32: 2.

Thine Eyes Shall See the King in His Beauty; They Shall Behold a Land That Reacheth Afar.

Isa. 33: 17.

And the Inhabitant Shall not Say, I am Sick: the People That Dwell Therein Shall be Forgiven Their Iniquity.

Isa. 33: 24.

STUDY TEN

A SERIES OF SIX WOES (CHAPTERS 28-33)

Woe to Drunken, Scoffing Politicians (Chapter 28)

1. This is one of the great chapters of Isaiah's book. It is the first of a series of six, all of which refer to the invasion of Sennacherib in 701 B. C. The opening verses (1-6), however, seem to have been first spoken before the downfall of Samaria (722 B. C.)—a hint possibly that the whole series may have been written earlier than is usually supposed (704-701 B. C.).

2. After pointing in warning to the proud drunkards of Ephraim, whose crown (Samaria) is rapidly fading (vs. 1-6), the prophet turns to the scoffing politicians of Jerusalem, rebuking especially the bibulous priests who stumble in judgment, and the staggering prophets who err in vision (vs. 7-8).

3. But they, looking up with bleared eyes, only mock in burlesque mimicry his monotonous preaching. (Each word in verse 10 is a monosyllable in Hebrew.) Whereupon, Isaiah hurls back the sarcastic but serious retort that Jehovah will one day speak to them in Assyrian monosyllables (vs. 11-13).

4. Then, without openly denouncing their desire to make an alliance with Egypt, he assures them that to suppose that they had made a "covenant with death" is a delusion, that judgment is imminent, and that the only true element of permanency in Zion is the "sure foundation" stone of faith (v. 16).

5. However, Jehovah's judgments upon them will not be arbitrary. The methods employed by peasants in agriculture are a parable of God's pur-

pose in disciplining. For example, the husbandman does not plow and harrow his fields the whole
year round; he plows and harrows that he may
also sow and reap. So God will not punish his people forever; a glorious future awaits the redeemed.
The husbandman does not thresh all kinds of grain
with equal severity; no more will God discipline
his people beyond their deserts (vs. 23-29).

Woe to Formalists in Religion (Chapter 29:1-14)

1. Isaiah's second woe is pronounced upon Ariel,
the altar-hearth of God, i. e., Jerusalem, the sacri-
ficial center of Israel's worship. David had first
inaugurated the true worship of Jehovah in Zion.
But now Zion's worship had become so formal and
heartless Jehovah determined with another full
year to allow Jerusalem to be besieged and fall
(vs. 1-4).

2. Not completely, however, for suddenly her
foes shall themselves be humiliated. Their prey
will elude them like the phantasm of a dream, and
they shall vanish. Shame and confusion will cover
them (vs. 5-8).

3. This is Jehovah's message to the masses. But
his nominal worshipers, who are spiritually blind
and therefore dull to comprehend the significance
of such words, stand and stare at the prophet as in
a stupor. Even the cultured fail to grasp the inner
meaning of the prophet's words; and as for the
unlearned, they gaze at him and his message as ignorant pagans stare at human handwriting (vs.
9-12).

4. The cause of such spiritual stupidity the
prophet declares to be their formality and hypocrisy in worship. Religion has become wholly
conventional and therefore insincere; it is learned

by rote (v. 13; cf. 1: 10-15; Mic. 6: 6-8). They draw nigh to Jehovah with their lips, while their hearts are far from him. Therefore, says Isaiah, Jehovah is forced to do an extraordinary work among them, in order to bring them back to a true knowledge of himself (v. 14).

Woe to Those Who hide their Plans from God (Chapter 29:15-24)

1. Isaiah's third woe is pronounced against those who secretly hide their counsel from Jehovah in order to avoid Jehovah's rebuke; who work in the dark, foolishly fancying that Jehovah does not see them (v. 15).

2. What their counsel is, or what they may be devising in secret, the prophet does not yet disclose; but he doubtless alludes to their intrigues with the Egyptians and their purpose to break faith with the Assyrians, to whom they were bound by treaty to pay annual tribute.

3. Isaiah bravely remonstrates with them for supposing that any policy will succeed which excludes the counsel and wisdom of the Holy One. They are but clay; he is the potter. Shall the creature attempt to dictate to the Creator? Can they by their cleverness correct his ways (v. 16; cf. 45: 9; 64: 8)?

4. At this point, though somewhat abruptly, Isaiah turns his face toward the Messianic future. In a very little while, he says, Lebanon, which is now overrun by Assyria's army, shall become a fruitful field, and the blind and deaf and spiritually weak shall rejoice in the Holy One of Israel; for the Assyrian tyrant shall be brought to nought, and Jerusalem's scoffing politicians shall be cut off (vs. 17-21).

5. The end of Israel's history shall be like its

beginning. As God ransomed Abraham from his heathen compatriots, so will Jehovah rescue Jacob-Israel from their idolatrous surroundings. Those capable of reformation will be reformed; those erring will be corrected; those given to murmuring will be admonished; while all will in that day submit docilely to the revealed teaching of God (vs. 22-24).

Woe to the Pro-Egyptian Party (Chapter 30)

1. Isaiah's fourth woe is directed against the rebellious politicians who stubbornly, and now openly, advocate making a league with Egypt. They have at length succeeded apparently in winning the king over to their side, and an embassy is already on its way to Egypt, bearing across the desert of the Exodus rich treasures with which to purchase the friendship of their former oppressors (vs. 1-5).

2. Isaiah now condemns what he can no longer prevent. He warns them that their policy is untheocratic because they lack faith in Jehovah, and therefore doomed to failure; that they absurdly exaggerate Egypt's resources; that they are grossly ignorant of Egypt's true character in time of war and danger; that Egypt is a Rahab "sit-still," i. e., a mythological sea monster menacing in mien but laggard in action; and that when the crisis comes she will sit still, causing Israel only shame and confusion (vs. 6-7).

3. But the advocates of the pro-Egyptian party stubbornly refuse to give heed to Isaiah's admonition. Accordingly Jehovah bids the prophet to take a tablet and to write before them in a book his unavailing protest against this fatal step, that it may be a perpetual memorial to the generations

to come of Judah's unwillingness to listen to Jehovah's instruction, forever and ever (vs. 8-14).

4. Therefore, urges the prophet, recall the embassy now on its way to Egypt, and trust quietly in Jehovah for deliverance in the impending crisis (vs. 15-17). Jehovah is waiting to be gracious. If Israel will only repent of their idolatry (vs. 18-26), copious blessings will follow and they "shall have a song as in the night" from the Rock of Israel (vs. 27-29).

5. But with fire and tempest he will suddenly devour the Assyrians, and kindle as with brimstone their funeral pile (vs. 30-33).

Woe to Those Who Trust in Horses and Chariots (Chapters 31-32)

1. Isaiah's fifth woe is a still more vehement denunciation of those who trust in Egypt's horses and chariots, and disregard the Holy One of Israel. Those who do this forget that the Egyptians are but men and their horses flesh, and that flesh cannot avail in a conflict with spirit (31: 1-3).

2. For it is Jehovah who, by means of Assyria, has seized hold of Jerusalem and like a lion holds it in his grasp; and it is idle folly to suppose that a few Egyptian allies, called in to help shepherd Jerusalem, will be able to scare the All-powerful One from his prey (31: 4). Note the Homeric ring of this verse!

3. Eventually Jehovah means to deliver Jerusalem, if the children of Israel will but turn from their idolatries to him; and in that day, Assyria will be vanquished (31: 5-9).

4. A new era will dawn upon Judah. Society will be regenerated. King and nobles will rule in righteousness, and the poor will find justice. The renovation of society will begin at the top. Those

who were once spiritually blind and deaf shall at length understand; those who thought aforetime only superficially, will think deeply; and those who stammered when speaking on religion, will henceforth speak clearly and forcibly. Conscience also will be sharpened, and moral distinctions will no longer be confused (32: 1-8). " The aristocracy of birth and wealth will be replaced by an aristocracy of character." (Delitzsch.)

5. The careless and indifferent women, too, in that day will no longer menace the social welfare of the state. Within a year their palaces and pleasant gardens will have been given over to wild asses and flocks for pasture. " Next year's harvests will never come " (32: 9-14; cf. 3: 16—4: 1).

6. With the outpouring of Jehovah's spirit an ideal commonwealth will emerge, in which social righteousness, peace, plenty and security will abound (32: 15-20).

Woe to the Assyrian Destroyer (Chapter 33)

1. Isaiah's last woe is directed against the treacherous spoiler himself, who has already laid waste the cities of Judah, and is now beginning to lay siege to Jerusalem (701 B. C.).

2. The precise historical situation of this chapter is defined in verses 7-12, from which it appears that the ambassadors, who were sent by Hezekiah with costly tribute to Sennacherib at Lachish, have returned home with the melancholy news that the treacherous Assyrian has accepted their tribute but refused to abandon the siege (cf. 2 Kings 18: 14-16). For Isaiah, such treachery fills the measure of Assyria's iniquity to the full, and the hour of Judah's deliverance is come (v. 10).

3. The prophet prays (v. 2); and while he prays, behold! the mighty hosts of the Assyrians are

routed, and the long-besieged but now triumphant inhabitants of Jerusalem rush out like locusts upon the spoil which the vanishing adversary has been forced to leave behind (vs. 3-4). The destroyer's plan to reduce Jerusalem has come to naught.

4. The whole earth beholds the spectacle of Assyria's defeat and is filled with awe and amazement at the mighty work of Jehovah. Even the sinners within Jerusalem stand aghast at Jehovah's omnipotence, and solemnly inquire: Who among us dare dwell in a city with such a God? Jehovah's wrath is like a divine fire, and his furnace is in Zion (v. 14; cf. 31: 9).

5. Only the righteous may henceforth dwell in Jerusalem. Their eyes shall behold the Messiah-king in his beauty, reigning no longer like Hezekiah over a limited and restricted territory, but over a land unbounded, whose inhabitants enjoy Jehovah's peace and protection, and are free from all sickness, and therefore from all sin (vs. 17-24). With this beautiful picture of the Messianic future, the prophet's woes find an appropriate conclusion.

Summary: No Woe without a Promise

1. The most striking feature of these prophecies is the constant alteration of threat and promise. Isaiah never pronounced a woe without adding a corresponding promise: thus, Woe to those who vainly scoff at Jehovah's warnings (28: 7-22); yet, God will not ruthlessly destroy even scoffers; he will only punish them according to their deserts (28: 23-29).

2. Woe to those who in their spiritual blindness and hypocrisy trust in form and ritual (29: 9-13); yet in order to rouse them from their spiritual stupor, God will do an extraordinary work and de-

stroy their arch-enemy without assistance (29: 5-8, 14).

3. Woe to those who exclude God from their plans and purposes, and practically dictate to their Creator what the issues of life must be (29: 15-16); yet even to such God will continue to reveal himself in wisdom and instruction (29: 17-24).

4. Woe to those who make friends with God's enemies, rejecting the counsel of his Spirit; who silence the voice of prophecy and demand that the seers preach " smooth things " (30: 10); yet even to them a voice will be heard from behind whispering, " This is the way, walk ye in it " (30: 21).

5. Woe to those who rely for help on flesh and blood rather than upon the spirit of the living God (31: 1, 3); yet such may be saved by repentance (31: 6), and be allowed to dwell in peace in a land rejuvenated by God's presence (32: 15-20).

6. Finally, woe to the treacherous enemies of the kingdom of God, who would violently destroy the last vestige of Jehovah's possessions; they shall be destroyed, and that without mercy (33: 1-12); on the other hand Israel will be gloriously delivered, and their iniquities forgiven (33: 22-24).

Thus Saith Jehovah, Set Thy House in Order; for Thou Shalt Die, and not Live.

Isa. 38: 1.

What Shall I Say? He Hath Both Spoken unto Me, and Himself Hath Done It: I Shall go Softly all My Years because of the Bitterness of My Soul. O Lord, by These Things Men Live; and Wholly Therein is the Life of My Spirit: Wherefore Recover Thou Me, and Make Me to Live.

Isa. 38: 15, 16.

STUDY ELEVEN

HISTORY, PROPHECY AND SONG
(CHAPTERS 36-39)

The Fourteenth Year of King Hezekiah
(Chapter 36:1)

1. In chapters 36-39 three important historical events are narrated, in which Isaiah was a prominent factor: (1) the double attempt of Sennacherib to obtain possession of Jerusalem (chapters 36-37); (2) Hezekiah's sickness and recovery (chapter 38); (3) the embassy of Merodach-Baladan (chapter 39). With certain omissions and insertions these chapters are duplicated verbatim in 2 Kings 18: 13—20: 19.

2. Chronologically chapters 38-39 precede chapters 36-37. This is probably due to the fact that chapters 36-37, which describe the siege of Jerusalem by Sennacherib in 701 B. C., explain and appropriately conclude chapters 1-35; whereas, chapters 38-39, which record Hezekiah's sickness (714 B. C.) and Merodach-Baladan's embassy of congratulation upon his recovery (712 B. C.), fittingly introduce chapters 40-66.

3. The whole section (chapters 36-39) is introduced with the chronological note, " Now it came to pass in the fourteenth year of king Hezekiah." Various attempts have been made to solve the mystery of this date; for if the author is alluding to the siege of 701 B. C., difficulty arises, because that event occurred not in Hezekiah's fourteenth but twenty-sixth year, according to the Biblical chronology; or if, with George Adam Smith and others, we date Hezekiah's accession to the throne of Judah as " most probably" in 720 B. C., then the siege of 701 B. C. occurred, as is evident, in Hezekiah's nineteenth year. It is barely possible that " the

fourteenth year of king Hezekiah " was the fourteenth of the fifteen years which were added to his
life, but more probably it alludes to the fourteenth
of his reign.

4. On the whole it is better to take the phrase as
a general chronological caption for the entire section, with special reference to chapter 38, which
tells of Hezekiah's sickness, which actually fell in
his fourteenth year (714 B. C.), and which, coupled
with Sargon's expected presence at Ashdod, was
the great personal crisis of the king's life.   In any
case the author of these chapters was not a mere
historian but a prophet.

The Events of 701 B.C. (Chapters 36-37)

1.   Sennacherib made two attempts in 701 B. C.
to reduce Jerusalem: one from Lachish with an
army (36: 2—37: 8), and another from Libnah
with a threat conveyed by messengers (37: 9-38).
The brief section contained in 2 Kings 18: 14-16 is
omitted from between verses 1 and 2 of Isaiah 36,
because it was not the prophet's aim at this time
to recount the nation's humiliation.

2. Sennacherib's two attempts to take Jerusalem
followed each other in rapid succession. First (36:
2—37: 8) he sent his commander-in-chief, the
Rabshakeh, from Lachish with a vast army (36:
2).   After arriving at Jerusalem, the Rabshakeh,
in an oral address in Hebrew before the walls of
the city, insolently defied Hezekiah and Hezekiah's
God (36: 13-20).   The king was panic-stricken.
He rent his clothes, repaired to the temple, and
sent a request to Isaiah to pray for the remnant of
his people (37: 1-4); whereupon Isaiah returned
answer that the king should not be afraid, for

Sennacherib would hear tidings and return to his own land (37: 5-7).

3. Sennacherib's second attempt (37: 9-38) was baffled by the rumored approach of Tirhakah, king of Ethiopia. Not being able to spare a detachment of the regular army he sends messengers to Hezekiah with an insulting letter, in which he threatens Jerusalem with utter destruction (37: 9-13). Hezekiah receives the letter and again repairs to the temple, spreads the letter before Jehovah that He may more clearly behold its arrogant character, and prays that Jehovah may vindicate himself as the only true and living God by saving the city (37: 14-20); whereupon Isaiah sends him a message of comfort, predicting that Sennacherib will not return to renew the siege, nor shoot an arrow into the city, and that the city will be surely delivered (37: 21-35).

4. It is then recorded (37: 36-37) how the angel of Jehovah went forth and smote, perhaps by means of a pestilence, as Herodotus suggests, 185,000 of Sennacherib's army, and how the king himself returned to Nineveh; to which an editor has appended the information that Sennacherib died a violent death at the hands of his two sons (37: 38). This happened twenty years subsequent to the siege of Jerusalem (681 B. C.); during all these years Sennacherib apparently never made another expedition into Palestine.

Isaiah's Last "Word" Concerning Assyria (Chapter 37:21-35)

1. This last formal prophecy concerning Assyria is one of Isaiah's grandest predictions. It was delivered during the din and excitement of a real crisis (701 B. C.), and before the historical issue was generally known.

2. It is composed of three parts: (1) A taunt-song in elegiac rhythm, on the inevitable humiliation of Sennacherib (vs. 22-29); (2) a short poem in different rhythm, directed to Hezekiah, in order to encourage his faith (vs. 30-32); (3) a definite prediction, in less elevated style, of the sure deliverance of Jerusalem (vs. 33-35).

3. The taunting tone of the first section (vs. 22-29) is accounted for by the insolent character of Sennacherib's letter (37: 10-13), in which he scorns the God of Israel as impotent and powerless to protect Jerusalem. Isaiah, on the contrary, reminds Sennacherib that Assyria's successes in time past were not due to their own gods, but rather to the eternal purpose of Jehovah, who has been using Assyria as an elect instrument in the overthrow of nations (37: 26; cf. 22: 11; 10: 5-15).

4. Then turning to King Hezekiah, in verses 30-32 Isaiah gives him a "sign," by which he may verify the prophetic "word." For two years there will not be regular harvests, but in the third, the surviving remnant will sow and reap in peace. Thus would Isaiah give the king a tangible support to faith, and encourage him in rejecting Sennacherib's insolent demand to surrender.

5. The prophecy concludes with a definite prediction of Jerusalem's deliverance (vs. 33-35), which was absolutely and literally fulfilled. " Never had a prophet predicted more boldly, never was a prediction more brilliantly fulfilled."

The Destruction of Sennacherib

The Assyrian came down like a wolf on the fold,
And his cohorts were gleaming in purple and gold;
And the sheen of their spears was like stars on the sea,
When the blue waves roll lightly on deep Galilee.

Like the leaves of the forest when Summer is green,
That host with their banners at sunset were seen:
Like the leaves of the forest when Autumn hath blown,
That host on the morrow lay wither'd and strown.

For the Angel of Death spread his wings on the blast,
And breathed in the face of the foe as he pass'd;
And the eyes of the sleepers wax'd deadly and chill,
And their hearts but once heaved, and forever grew
    still:

And there lay the steed with his nostril all wide,
But through it there roll'd not the breath of his pride;
And the foam of his gasping lay white on the turf,
And cold as the spray of the rock-beating surf.

And there lay the rider distorted and pale,
With the dew on his brow, and the rust on his mail:
And the tents were all silent, the banners alone,
The lances unlifted, the trumpets unblown.

And the widows of Asshur are loud in their wail,
And the idols are broke in the temple of Baal;
And the might of the Gentile, unsmote by the sword,
Hath melted like snow at the glance of the Lord!

                        —Lord Byron.

Hezekiah's Sickness and Recovery (Chapter 38)

1. " In those days (i. e., his fourteenth year, 714 B. C.) was Hezekiah sick unto death." The king was about thirty-eight years of age when Isaiah was divinely commanded to pronounce upon him the sentence of death: " Set thy house in order; for thou shalt die and not live " (v. 1).

2. Hezekiah at that time had no son (39: 7; cf. 2 Kings 21: 1), and the dynasty of David, in which centered so many Messianic hopes, was seriously threatened. The king accordingly turned his face to the wall and prayed and wept sore; whereupon Jehovah, seeing Hezekiah's tears, revoked his death sentence, and added to his life fifteen years (vs. 2-5).

3. God also gave him a " sign " that what he promised would come to pass. As Hezekiah lay in his palace chamber he could look through the window and watch the sun's shadow descend on the staircase of Ahaz, by which the king was accustomed to go up into the house of the Lord (cf. 1 Kings 10: 5). The shadow naturally would serve the purpose of a chronometer for the dying monarch. That the shadow might be an indubitable sign to Hezekiah, God caused it to return backward "ten steps." So the sun returned "ten steps" on the dial, or steps, whereon it was gone down (vs. 6-8).

4. Among the celebrated sun-dials of antiquity this staircase of Ahaz has become the most famous. That of Augustus on the field of Mars in Rome is another. There is a modern dial on the rear of the Sirdar's palace at Khartum in the Sudan, which bears the suggestive motto: " The bird of time has but a little way to fly, And lo! the bird is on the wing."

5. The prophet's prescription for the king's malady in verses 21-22, which in 2 Kings 20 stands after verse 6, comes in rather awkwardly after Hezekiah's psalm, but its position may be due to the editor's desire to bring verses 20 and 22 into close juxtaposition.

Hezekiah's Song of Thanksgiving (Chapter 38:9-20)

1. This beautiful plaintive " Writing " of King Hezekiah, in which he celebrates his recovery from some mortal sickness, expresses the sentiments and feelings of one who has himself personally been unexpectedly and miraculously delivered from the brink of death. It is omitted altogether by the author of the book of Kings (cf. 2 Kings 20).

2. With hopeless melancholy the king, in the first half of the poem, depicts his deep despondency when confronting death and the darkness of Sheol (vs. 10-14); but with correspondingly boundless rapture he describes his joy at the thought of continued life in communion with Jehovah in the land of the living (vs. 15-20).

3. A more minute outline of this royal psalm is as follows: (1) Verses 10-12 review the king's feelings as in the noontide of life (thirty-eight years old) he faced gloomy Sheol, whose pale inhabitants were supposed in Old Testament times to lose all interest in human affairs and to be completely cut off from all conscious communion with God. (2) Verses 13-14 describe how in the midst of his distress he prayed, but God did not regard him; and how sometimes during his illness he felt so languid that he despaired of living out the day. (3) Verses 15-17 relate how Jehovah came to his rescue, and not only promised him life but actually caused him to live. Therefore, he asks, What can I render to God for his faithfulness? I shall go softly, as in solemn procession, all my added years; for now I see that my affliction was God's chastisement, and that by such experiences and with the help of such promises, men really live. (4) In verses 18-20, he continues to rejoice in the prospect of continued communion with God in the land of the living; and vows that as a faithful choragus he will sing songs with which to celebrate Jehovah's praise in the temple all the remaining days of his life (cf. 2 Chron. 29: 30).

4. While Hezekiah's view of the future world is gloomy, being without consciousness of God's presence, and consequently without moral or intellectual energy (v. 18), yet the same view is entertained in several of the psalms (6: 5; 55: 4; 56: 13; 116: 3), and is in perfect harmony with Hezekiah's early times.

The Embassy of Merodach-Baladan (Chapter 39)

1. Hezekiah was sick in 714 B. C. Two years later Merodach-Baladan, the veteran arch-enemy of Assyria, having heard of his wonderful recovery, sent letters and a present to congratulate him (v. 1).

2. Doubtless also political motives prompted the recalcitrant Babylonian. Sargon complains in one of his inscriptions that Merodach-Baladan was ever sending ambassadors to the disaffected subjects of the empire, inciting them to join with him in getting rid of the Assyrian yoke. The chronicler mentions scientific curiosity as another motive for the embassy (2 Chron. 32: 31).

3. In any case Hezekiah was greatly flattered by the visit of Merodach-Baladan's envoys; and, in a moment of weakness, showed them all his royal treasures (v. 2). This was an inexcusable blunder, as the sight of his many precious possessions would only excite Babylonian cupidity to possess Jerusalem.

4. Isaiah at once perceived the issues of the transaction and sought an interview with Hezekiah. In tones of prophetic authority he catechized the king as to the ambassadors, their home, what they had said, and what they had seen, and boldly rebuked him for his vanity of heart and lack of faith in Jehovah in thus receiving them. And not only did he solemnly condemn the king's conduct, but he announced with more than ordinary insight that the days were coming when all the accumulated resources of Jerusalem would be carried away to Babylon (vs. 3-6; cf. Mic. 4: 10).

5. Hezekiah, conscience-smitten, in pious resignation meekly submitted to the prophet's rebuke; evidently, however, regarding the postponement of the calamity as a mitigation of its severity (vs. 7-8).

6. This final prediction of judgment is the most marvelous of all Isaiah's minatory utterances; because he distinctly asserts that, not the Assyrians, who were then at the height of their power, but the Babylonians, shall be the instruments of the divine vengeance in consummating Jerusalem's destruction. There is absolutely no reason for doubting the genuineness of this prediction. In it we have a prophetic basis for chapters 40-66, which follow.

An Estimate of Hezekiah

1. Hezekiah is mentioned thirty-one times in Isaiah 36-39. Next to David he was the greatest king the Jews ever had. Throughout his entire reign Isaiah was his constant counselor.

2. His deeds were important and manifold. He began his reign with a widespread reformation of religion, and renovation and purification of the temple and its services (2 Kings 18: 4; cf. 2 Chron. 29-30); he built a pool and an aqueduct to improve the water supply of Jerusalem (2 Kings 20: 20); he encouraged and promoted literature (Prov. 25: 1); in short, he did that which was right as David his father had done, so that neither before nor after him was there a king like him (2 Kings 18: 5; cf. however 23: 25). Jesus Ben-Sirach associates him with David and Josiah (Ecclus. 48: 22; 49: 4).

3. In his sickness he learned the true meaning of life, and was led to interpret God's discipline in terms of wisdom and love (Isa. 38: 17). In consequence of his vain display of his riches to the Babylonian envoys, he learned humility (2 Chron. 32: 25-26); while by his rebellion against Assyria (2 Kings 18: 7), he brought upon him and his people a series of events which taught him that the highest type of patriotism was faith in Jehovah-God. The secret of his life was prayer.

4. Side by side for nearly thirty years, the king and the prophet guided the ship of state, and by God's mercy Jerusalem was saved.

COMFORT YE, COMFORT YE MY PEOPLE, SAITH YOUR GOD.

Isa. 40: 1.

THE VOICE OF ONE THAT CRIETH, PREPARE YE IN THE WILDERNESS THE WAY OF JEHOVAH; MAKE LEVEL IN THE DESERT A HIGHWAY FOR OUR GOD.

Isa. 40: 3.

TO WHOM THEN WILL YE LIKEN ME, THAT I SHOULD BE EQUAL TO HIM? SAITH THE HOLY ONE.

Isa. 40: 25.

BUT THEY THAT WAIT FOR JEHOVAH SHALL RENEW THEIR STRENGTH; THEY SHALL MOUNT UP WITH WINGS AS EAGLES; THEY SHALL RUN AND NOT BE WEARY; THEY SHALL WALK, AND NOT FAINT.

Isa. 40: 31.

STUDY TWELVE

DELIVERANCE FROM CAPTIVITY THROUGH CYRUS (CHAPTERS 40-48)

The Basic of Comfort, Israel's Incomparable God (Chapter 40)

1. We now pass to the great theme, so often enunciated by Isaiah, of Israel's redemption. The mass of Judah and all North Israel are in exile. It is not necessary, however, to suppose that *all* Judah have gone into captivity, or that the author himself was one of those carried away; much less that one hundred and fifty years elapsed between chapters 39 and 40. Sennacherib had stripped Judah bare and had almost captured Jerusalem in 701 B. C.

2. Postulate a prophet, therefore, who like Isaiah was constantly looking for comfort to the future (1: 27-28; 2: 2-4; 6: 13; 7: 16; 8: 4; 10: 20-23; 11: 6-16; 17: 14; 18: 7; 19: 19-25; 26: 20; 29: 5, 17-24; 30: 31; 31: 8; 32: 16-20; 33: 17-24; 35: 10; 37: 26-29, 33-35; 38: 5-6) and chapters 40ff. find a most satisfactory setting at the close of the eighth century B. C. The problem of prime importance before the prophet's mind would naturally be to explain why Jehovah, the Holy One of Israel, allowed His own chosen people to be thus humiliated.

3. He begins by pointing Israel to the infinite, all-wise, and all-powerful Jehovah, who, in comparison with other gods is incomparable (chapter 40). His logic is absolutely unanswerable.

4. In the prologue (40: 1-11), he hears the four voices of grace (vs. 1-2), prophecy (vs. 3-5), faith (vs. 6-8), and evangelism (vs. 9-11).

5. In verses 12-26 he describes the unique character of Israel's all but forgotten God. Jehovah, he

unhesitatingly affirms, is infinite as compared with
the created world (vs. 12-17), with other gods (vs.
18-20), or with the stars (vs. 21-26).

6. Therefore, let no man suppose that Jehovah
is ignorant of, or indifferent to, Israel's misery.
The Holy One never faints nor wearies. On the
contrary, he it is who sustains the faint and
strengthens the weary. Israel must wait for salvation. They are clamoring for deliverance pre-
maturely. Only wait, he repeats; for, with such
a God Israel has no reason to despond (vs. 27-31).

The Supreme Proof of Jehovah's Sole Deity, His Power to Predict (Chapter 41)

1. In chapter 40 the prophet had pointed to the
wonderful works of creation as evidence of Jehovah's incomparable power and greatness; here in
chapter 41, he challenges the nations to a public
trial, in order that, not by an appeal to contemporary history, as some suppose, but by predicting
a definite epoch-making event, which shall take
place in the future, he may demonstrate Jehovah's
sole deity, and therefore, his incomparable superiority to dumb idols.

2. He inquires, " Who hath raised up one from
the east?" Though the hero is left unnamed,
Cyrus is doubtless in the prophet's mind (44: 28;
45: 1). He is not, however, *already* appearing upon the horizon of history, as is sometimes fancied,
but rather predicted as sure to come. The verb-
tenses which express completed action are perfects
of certainty, and are used in precisely the same
manner as those in 3: 8; 5: 13; 21: 9. The answer to the inquiry is, " I, Jehovah, the first, and
with the last, I am he " (41: 4).

3. The prophet pauses to assure Israel of Jehovah's help. Israel is here for the first time called

Jehovah's " servant," a relation which he has sustained to Jehovah ever since Abraham's call from " the ends of the earth," i. e., from Babylon, which is spoken of as a far-distant country to the author (41: 8, 9).

4. At this point the dialogue shifts; it is no longer between Jehovah and the nations as in verses 1-7, but between Jehovah and the idols (vs. 21-29). Addressing the dumb idols Jehovah says: Predict something, if you are real deities (vs. 21-24). As for myself, I am going to raise up a hero from the north who will subdue all who oppose him. And I announce my purpose now in advance, " from the beginning," "beforetime," before there is the slightest ground for thinking that such a hero exists or ever will exist (v. 26), in order that the future may verify my prediction, and prove my sole deity. I, Jehovah, alone know the future. In verses 25-29, the prophet even projects himself into the future and speaks from the standpoint of the fulfilment of his prediction. This, as we have seen, was a characteristic of Isaiah (cf. chapters 24-27).

The Spiritual Agent of Redemption, Jehovah's "Servant" (Chapters 42:1 — 43:13)

1. Not only a temporal agent (Cyrus) shall be raised up to mediate Israel's redemption, which is the first step in the process of the universal salvation contemplated, but a spiritual factor, Jehovah's "servant," shall be employed in bringing the good tidings of salvation to the Gentiles also.

2. In 42: 1-9 the prophet describes this ideal figure and the work he is called to execute: Jehovah's Spirit will rest upon him, he will teach the world true religion, he will restore Israel, and bring justice and light to the Gentiles, and his advent will be a definite guarantee of Jehovah's predictions,

3. The glorious future evokes a brief hymn of thanksgiving for the redemption which the prophet beholds in prospect (42: 10-17). The time to redeem Israel is now come; Jehovah's glory is at stake (42: 8, 12); otherwise the heathen will claim that their gods have permanently wrested Israel out of Jehovah's hands.

4. The philosophy of events is this: though Israel have long served as Jehovah's "servants," yet they have been blind and deaf to Jehovah's instructions (42: 18-19), and he has found it necessary to punish them (42: 22); but now he will redeem Israel that, through them, he may publish his law to all nations (42: 21); if they will but " harken and hear for the time to come " (42: 23).

5. To accomplish this end, Jehovah will ransom Israel at the cost of the most opulent and powerful nations of the world—Egypt, Ethiopia and Seba— and will gather them from the four corners of the earth (43: 1-7; cf. 11: 11ff).

6. Let the nations therefore come again together for the trial. Who of them dare definitely predict the redemption of Israel? But, says Jehovah, even you who are blind can bear witness that I have often foretold coming events which have actually come to pass (cf. 37: 26); I alone can do it. Besides me there is no Saviour (43: 8-13). The prophet throughout professes to be foretelling future events.

Forgiveness, Jehovah's Pledge of Deliverance (Chapters 43:14 — 44:23)

1. The prophet announces the fate of Babylon; in most general terms, however. He merely intimates that Israel's present oppressors shall no more prevent Jehovah from carrying out his redemptive plan than Pharaoh in Moses' time was able to thwart their exodus from Egypt. The new exodus, indeed, will eclipse the former in glory (43: 14-21).

2. Jehovah's determination to redeem Israel is all of grace; the exiles have done nothing worthy of so great redemption. They have offered neither prayer nor sacrifices of any kind. Jehovah has blotted out their transgressions for his own sake (43: 25). Salvation is a gift. "This passage marks the highest point of grace in the Old Testament." (Dillmann.)

3. Filled with Jehovah's Spirit Israel will subsequently attract the nations (44: 1-5). Jehovah is King as well as Redeemer. His sole deity is attested by his power to predict future events; he has done so in the past and he can do so now. Future events are known to him alone (44: 6-8). His prophecies will have special value when they have been fulfilled. There is no Rock like Israel's God.

4. Gods of wood and stone are nonentities. The prophet takes his reader into an idol manufactury, and shows him how the smiths and carpenters, with axes and hammers, planes and compasses, hew out of cedar trees and oaks gods before which they bow down and worship; the residue of which they use as fuel. Such people, he unhesitatingly affirms, are blind and dull of heart, and are "feeding on ashes." The passage as a whole is a most remorseless exposure of the folly of idolatry (44: 9-20).

5. Finally he exhorts: Above all else, let Israel remember that forgiveness is Jehovah's pledge of deliverance (44: 21-23).

Cyrus, Jehovah's Agent in Israel's Deliverance (Chapters 44:24 — 45:25)

1. The prophet at length names the hero—Cyrus,

and describes his mission: he shall build Jerusalem and lay the foundations of the temple (44: 28); he shall also subdue nations and let the exiles go free (45: 1, 13). These minute specifications were necessary in order to make his predictions definite and certain, and so prove his thesis.

2. He speaks of Cyrus in the most extraordinary, almost extravagant, terms. He is Jehovah's "shepherd" (44: 28)—"the name Cyrus in Elamite is said to mean shepherd " (A. B. Davidson); he is also Jehovah's " anointed," i. e., Messiah (45: 1), "the man of my counsel" (46: 11), whom Jehovah has called by name, and surnamed without his ever knowing him (45: 3-4); " whom Jehovah loveth " (48: 14), whose right hand Jehovah upholdeth (45: 1), and who will perform all Jehovah's pleasure (45: 28); though but " a ravenous bird from the east " (46: 11).

3. The vividness with which the prophet speaks of Cyrus leads some to suppose that the latter is already upon the horizon. This, however, is a mistake. Scarcely would a contemporary have spoken in such terms of the real Cyrus of 538 B. C. The same prophecy regards him (i. e., the Cyrus of prediction; not the Cyrus of history) as the fulfilment of predictions spoken long before. That is to say, in one and the same context, Cyrus is both predicted and treated as a proof that a prediction is in him being fulfilled (44: 24-28; 45: 21). Such phenomena in prophecy can be explained best by supposing that the prophet projected himself into the future from an earlier age. Isaiah frequently did so, as we have seen in chapters 24-27.

4. Most extraordinary of all, in 45: 14-17, the prophet soars in imagination until he sees, as a result of Cyrus' victories, the conquered nations renouncing their idols, and attracted to Jehovah as the Saviour of all mankind (45: 22). On any theory of origin, the predictive element in these prophecies is written large.

5. Josephus tells us that when Cyrus found his name written in " the prophecies which Isaiah left behind him two hundred and twenty years before, an earnest desire and ambition seized upon him to fulfill what was written " (*Antiquities*, XI., 1, 2).

The Overthrow of Babylon (Chapters 46-47)

1. Chapters 46-47 further describe the destructive work of Cyrus, though Cyrus himself is but once referred to. Particular emphasis is laid on the complete collapse of the Babylonian religion; the prophet is apparently more concerned with the humiliation of Babylon's idols than with the fall of the city itself. Of course the destruction of the city would imply the defeat of her gods, as also the emancipation of Israel.

2. The prophet draws a striking contrast between the ignominious flight of Babylon's idols, borne into exile from the captured city on the backs of wearied beasts, and the matchless power of Jehovah, who, instead of being borne, is able to bear His people. Even Bel, the chief god of the Babylonian pantheon, and Nebo, the interpreter of the gods, are powerless to help (46: 1-2).

3. The proof which is given again in support of Jehovah's incomparable superiority and unique deity, is His power to predict " the end from the beginning " and bring his predictions to pass (46: 10-11). With unwonted severity he addresses his hearers as, " transgressors " (46: 8), and " stouthearted that are far from righteousness" (46: 12); yet in spite of them, salvation is the determined goal of coming events (46: 13).

4. Chapter 47 is a dirge over the downfall of the imperial city, strongly resembling the taunt-song

on the king of Babylon in 14: 4-21. Babylon is
addressed as a " tender and delicate " queen, the
mistress of kingdoms, who because of her boastful-
ness and cruelty, will be dethroned and led into
captivity to a distant land and there made to grind
as a slave behind the millstones (47: 1-7).

5. No amount of sorcery or enchantment or
science of astrology will suffice to avert the divine
desolation which will one day fall upon the haughty capital (47: 8-15).

A Hortatory Summary of the Argument (Chapter 48)

1. Chapter 48 in the main is a brief recapitula-
tion of the arguments insisted on in chapters 40-
47; certain points being touched upon and emphasized for the last time:

(1) Jehovah's unique power to predict. Let the
house of Jacob know and understand that Jehovah's method of predicting future events and ful-
filling his predictions has been vindicated by history over and over again, some predictions having
been announced long in advance, others on the eve
of their accomplishment; yea, and that his new
prediction concerning the redemption of Israel
will also be vindicated, for he will surely bring it
to pass. Idols are nonentities (48: 1-8).

(2) That salvation is of grace. Let the house of
Jacob know also and understand that Israel's redemption is not for their sake but for Jehovah's;
" For mine own sake, for mine own sake, will I do
it " (48: 9-11).

(3) That Cyrus, as Jehovah's agent, will faithfully perform all his pleasure on Babylon. His advent will be the crowning proof of Jehovah's abid-
ing presence among his people. In order that the
evidence may be perfectly clear, Jehovah makes

bold to call him openly, " not in secret," and in advance of his advent, even " from the beginning," in order that men may be obliged to confess that God has done it, by his Spirit (48: 12-16).

(4) That God's chastisements upon the nation were intended to be disciplinary. For had Israel only learned the lessons which God was all along trying to teach them through their afflictions and sufferings, then had their peace been like a river, and their righteousness as the waves of the sea (48: 17-19).

(5) But even now, the prophet exhorts them to accept of Jehovah's proffered salvation; and he closes with a jubilant summons addressed to the believing exiles, bidding them to depart from Babylon and publish to all the world the story of their redemption. Alas! that there is no peace or salvation for the godless (48: 20-22).

2. Thus ends the first division of Isaiah's remarkable *vision* of Israel's deliverance fom captivity through Cyrus.

A Bruised Reed will He not Break, and a Dimly Burning Wick will He not Quench; He will Bring Forth Justice in Truth.

Isa. 42: 3.

Surely He Hath Borne Our Griefs, and Carried Our Sorrows: yet We did Esteem Him Stricken, Smitten of God, and Afflicted. But He was Wounded for Our Transgressions, He was Bruised for Our Iniquities; the Chastisement of Our Peace was upon Him; and with His Stripes We are Healed.

Isa. 53: 4, 5.

Ho, Every One That Thirsteth, Come Ye to the Waters, and He That Hath no Money; Come Ye, Buy, and Eat; Yea, Come, Buy Wine and Milk without Money and without Price.

Isa. 55: 1.

Seek Ye Jehovah while He may be Found; Call Ye upon Him while He is near: Let the Wicked Forsake His Way, and the Unrighteous Man His Thoughts; and Let Him Return unto Jehovah, and He will have Mercy upon Him; and to Our God, for He will Abundantly Pardon.

Isa. 55: 6, 7.

STUDY THIRTEEN

THE SERVANT OF JEHOVAH
(CHAPTERS 49-57)

The Prophetic Setting of the "Servant Songs"

1. With chapter 49 the prophet leaves off attempting further to prove the sole deity of Jehovah by means of prediction, and drops entirely his description of Cyrus' victories and the overthrow of Babylon, in order to set forth in greater detail the character and mission of the spiritual agent of salvation—the Servant of Jehovah.

2. Already, in chapters 40-48, he had alluded several times to this unique and somewhat enigmatical personage, speaking of him both collectively and as an individual (41: 8-10; 42: 1-9, 18-22; 43: 10; 44: 1-5, 21-28; 45: 4; 48: 20-22); but now he defines with greater precision both his prophetic and priestly functions, his equipment for his task, his sufferings and humiliation, and also his final exaltation. Altogether in these prophecies he mentions the Servant some twenty times.

3. There are four so-called distinctively " Servant Songs," in which the prophet seems to rise above the collective masses of all Israel to at least a personification of the pious within Israel, or, better, to a unique Person embodying within himself all that is best in the Israel within Israel. They are the following:

(1) Chapter 42: 1-9, a poem descriptive of the Servant's gentle manner and world-wide mission. This is followed, as we have seen in the previous Study, by prophecies concerning Cyrus and the fall of Babylon.

(2) Chapter 49: 1-13, describing the Servant's

mission and spiritual success; followed by promises of comfort to Zion (49: 14—50: 3).

(3) Chapter 50: 4-11, the Servant's soliloquy concerning his perfection through suffering; followed again by messages of comfort and encouragement to the believers in Zion (51: 1—52: 12).

(4) Chapters 52: 13—53: 12, the Servant's vicarious suffering and ultimate exaltation; followed by a vivid description of Zion's future prosperity and glory (chapter 54), and an urgent invitation to men immersed in business to accept of God's proffered salvation (chapter 55): even proselytes and eunuchs being allowed to share in the blessings of redemption (56: 1-8); the section closing with a scathing rebuke to faithless shepherds and sensual idolaters (56: 9—57: 21).

The First of the Four "Servant Songs" (Chapter 42:1-9)

1. The prophet had already prepared the way for a definite introduction of Jehovah's individual Servant, by designating "Israel" as Jehovah's Servant in 41: 8-16; describing him as having been chosen of God when Abraham was called from the ends of the earth, as being conscious of God's call, and as assured by Jehovah of glorious victory (41: 8-16). In this passage the entire nation seems to be present to the prophet's mind.

2. The first of the four distinctively "Servant Songs" is found in 42: 1-9. Several important features are mentioned in it as characteristic of the Servant's person and work. (1) His endowment: Jehovah puts his spirit upon him. (2) His mission: he will bring forth justice to the Gentiles, i. e., he will teach the nations honesty and righteousness. (3) His method: not violence, but

meekness and peace are the means which he employs to bring salvation. (4) His success: he will not fail or be discouraged till he has performed his entire mission. (5) His mediatorial office: a covenant of the people. " I, Jehovah, have called thee in righteousness, and will hold thy hand, and will keep thee, and give thee for a covenant of the people, for a light of the Gentiles " (42: 6).

3. If we inquire who this Servant is, our answer will depend largely on our opinion as to when the prophecy was composed. If chapters 40-66 are exilic (550-538 B. C.), then the Servant cannot well be an individual, but Israel collectively considered; on the other hand, if Isaiah wrote these oracles at the close of the eighth century B. C., then the Servant might consistently be conceived of, in vision, as arising from the sorrows of the exile already begun, even as Immanuel is conceived of by Isaiah as arising from the devastations of Assyria (chapters 7-8). To the present writer the latter is not only possible but probable.

The Second of the Four "Servant Songs" (Chapter 49:1-13)

1. It is somewhat confusing, after the lofty picture of the ideal and apparently individual Servant described in 42: 1-9, that the prophet should revert to *all* Israel as Jehovah's Servant, as in 42: 18-22; 43: 10; 44: 1-5, 21-28; 45: 4; 48: 20-22; for it is quite obvious that in all these passages he is alluding to the masses of the people as a whole, reproving, consoling, admonishing and reassuring them.

2. But he soon recovers himself; and in the second of the four "Servant Songs" (49: 1-13) makes a distinct advance over the first, in the development of the Servant's mission and experience. The

Servant is here a prophet, whose sphere is world-wide. Called by Jehovah from his mother's womb (49: 1, 5), given by him for a covenant of the people to gather Israel and re-allot to them their desolate land (49: 8), he will be a light also to the Gentiles (49: 6).

3. The song is the natural sequel to that in 42: 1-9. The new features are: (1) the Servant's consciousness of his mission (49: 1-3); (2) his confession of failure in the past (49: 4); and (3) his quickened faith in the revelation that Jehovah has raised him up for a still greater purpose, namely, to be his organ of salvation to the ends of the earth (49: 5-6). Yet he plainly sees that before he can perform his mission to the nations he must do a preliminary work for his own people.

4. If, again, we ask who the Servant in this second poem is, our decision will probably halt between Israel and a personification of the truly spiritual Israel; for in verse 3 " Israel " is explicitly declared to be Jehovah's Servant, whereas in verse 5 the Servant is distinguished from Israel as the redeemer of Israel. The dominant notes of the passage point to a personification.

The Third of the Four "Servant Songs" (Chapter 50:4-11)

1. In the third of these poems the Servant is introduced by the prophet as speaking of himself and his work in monologue or soliloquy. " The Lord Jehovah hath given me the tongue of them that are taught, that I may know how to sustain with words him that is weary " (50: 4).

2. Speaking thus in the first person the Servant describes the prophetic aspect of his own character. " He possesses the two fundamental qualifica-

tions of an ideal prophet: willingness to listen as
often as God speaks, and willingness always to utter without demur whatever God commands."
(Orelli.)

3. It is in this Song that we hear for the first
time of the bitter scorn and contumely through
which he is compelled to pass (50: 6-9); also, of
the patient manner in which, in the discharge of
his commission, he bore the abuse and insult
which were heaped upon him, ever sustained by a
steadfast faith in Jehovah's willingness to help.
On the other hand, the prophet adds, only retribu-
tion and sorrow await those who, refusing to listen
to God's ideal Servant, oppose him (50: 10-11).

4. In this Song, as in the first of the series, the
Servant is free from all national limitations. The
concept is not bound to Israel either in their total-
ity, or as a spiritual church. Rather the Servant is
portrayed as an individual, as a prophet, sinless,
and obedient to the divine will; submissively patient, because conscious of Jehovah's unfailing
support. In short, he is described as an ideal
prophet made perfect through sufferings.

5. The term " Servant " occurs but once only in
the poem, and then near its end (50: 10).

The Last of the Four "Servant Songs"
(Chapters 52:13 — 53:12)

1. In this fourth and last of the "Servant Songs"
(52: 13—53: 12), we reach the climax of the
prophet's inspired symphony, and the acme also
of Hebrew prophecy. The profoundest thoughts
in the Old Testament revelation are to be found in
this section. It is a vindication of the Servant, so
clear and so true, and wrought out with such a
pathos and potency, that it holds first place in
Messianic prophecy. So far as fact and accuracy

of description are concerned, it might well have been composed after the tragedy on Calvary. Polycarp called it " the golden passional of the Old Testament."

2. The chapter division at the end of 52: 15 is unfortunate; 52: 13-15 forms an integral portion of this beautiful and pathetic poem. It consists of five strophes of three verses each: the first of which describes the Servant's destiny (52: 13-15); the second, his career (53: 1-3); the third, his suffering (53: 4-6); the fourth, his submission (53: 7-9); the fifth, his reward (53: 10-12).

3. The idea of death is a new thought in this song (53: 7-9). In the previous songs the Servant had been described as a prophet; here he is pictured as a priest, vicariously suffering for the sins of others, "to whom the stroke was due " (53: 8). He is a sin-bearing martyr, meek and patient; a man of sorrows and acquainted with grief.

4. " He was despised and rejected of men " (53: 3). With this verse Handel opens the second part of his great oratorio, "The Messiah." It is said that at this point in its composition, he was found with his head upon the table, weeping. "He was wounded for our transgressions" (53: 5); concerning this verse, Spurgeon is said to have remarked, " I have lost the power to doubt him when I see those wounds."

5. The most striking feature of the prophet's portrait is the unparalleled sufferings of the Servant and the effect they produce on the minds of his contemporaries. " It is a most remarkable anticipation of the sufferings of Christ and the glory that should follow." (Skinner.)

6. Henceforth we hear no more of " the Servant of Jehovah," but of "the servants of Jehovah" (54: 17; 56: 6; 63: 17; 65: 8, 9, 13, 14, 15; 66: 14; cf. however 61: 1-3). The lesson is patent.

Who the Servant of Jehovah Is

1. Opinions vary. The popular view is that the suffering Servant of chapters 40-66 is the loyal, spiritual kernel of Israel personified.

2. Delitzsch's view is suggestive; namely, that the idea of the Servant of Jehovah, to speak figuratively, is a pyramid. The lowermost basis is the whole of Israel: the middle section, Israel after the Spirit; while the summit is the person of the Mediator of salvation arising out of Israel.

3. A. B. Davidson's view is also worthy of mention. According to it, the Servant is the hidden Israel within Israel, abstracted and personified as a being, conceived of not as a collective, but as a unity. The ideal of a Servant is primary, those in whom the ideal is incarnate are secondary. The prophet does not idealize the actual, he actualizes the ideal. In short, the Servant is a conception incarnated, a being which does not belong to the Israel of any particular age, but which is permanent.

4. But Davidson is frank to acknowledge that his view is bound up with the critical date which he assigns these prophecies, namely, just before the restoration under Cyrus (536 B. C.), and that from the point of view of the exile the Servant of Jehovah can hardly have been an individual. On the other hand, he allows, if Isaiah were the author, that " he might have looked forward to such a great individual and have placed his rise amidst the sorrows of the exile, just as in the earlier chapters, Immanuel appears to rise in the midst of the devastations caused by the Assyrian invasion." (*Old Testament Prophecy*, p. 440.)

5. Fortunately the difference between a person and a personification is not great. To the present

writer the Servant of Jehovah in these passages rises to the full stature of an individual.

The Fulfillment of these Prophecies in Christ

1. Whatever attitude we assume toward these oracles, whether as critics we are concerned only to discover what the prophet intended, or as theologians, we consider it of no consequence what subject the prophet actually had in mind, practically all are agreed that these predictions find their ultimate fulfilment in Christ.

2. When the evangelist Philip joined himself to the chariot of the Ethiopian eunuch, he heard him reading Isa. 53: 7-8, " He was led as a sheep to the slaughter; and as a lamb before his shearers is dumb, so he openeth not his mouth;" and when asked by the eunuch to explain the passage, " Philip opened his mouth and beginning from this scripture, preached unto him Jesus " (Acts 8: 26-35). The New Testament is the authoritative expounder of Messianic prophecy.

3. Speaking of the Servant in chapter 53, Prof. George Adam Smith says: " Whether this figure be of the pious portion of Israel or of one holy sufferer, the Christian church has been right in finding its fulfilment in Jesus Christ; in his sinless suffering, in his consciousness of his solitary distinction from his people; in his knowledge that his suffering was of God's will, and would effect the forgiveness of his people's sin, their redemption from guilt, and so his own exaltation from misunderstanding and abuse to manifest power and glory."

4. And Oehler makes the following general remark concerning these passages: " In these discourses the contemplation of the prophet ascends

by stages as it were from the foundation walls of a cathedral, inclosing a large space, to the giddy height of the towering summit upon which the Cross has been planted; and the nearer it approaches the summit, the clearer appears the outline of the Cross fixed there: arrived at top, it rests in peace, for it has reached what was desired when it began to ascend the first steps of the temple tower."

5. The Servant of Jehovah has been realized in the Son of Man.

Behold, Jehovah's Hand is not Shortened, That It cannot Save; neither His Ear Heavy, That It cannot Hear.

Isa. 59: 1.

Arise, Shine; for Thy Light is Come, and the Glory of Jehovah is Risen upon Thee.

Isa. 60: 1.

Who are These That Fly as a Cloud, and as the Doves to Their Windows?

Isa. 60: 8.

The Spirit of the Lord Jehovah is upon Me; because Jehovah Hath Anointed Me to Preach Good Tidings unto the Meek; He Hath Sent Me to Bind up the Broken Hearted, to Proclaim Liberty to the Captives, and the Opening of the Prison to Them That are Bound.

Isa. 61: 1.

Who is This That Cometh from Edom, with Dyed Garments from Bozrah? This that is Glorious in His Apparel, Marching in the Greatness of His Strength? I That Speak in Righteousness, Mighty to Save.

Isa. 63: 1.

STUDY FOURTEEN

THE FUTURE GLORY OF THE PEOPLE OF GOD (CHAPTERS 58-66)

True Fasting and Faithful Sabbath Observance (Chapter 58)

1. Having described in chapters 49-57 the spiritual agent of Israel's salvation, the Servant of Jehovah, the prophet proceeds in this last section (chapters 58-66) to define the conditions on which salvation may be enjoyed. He begins as in the two preceding sections (chapters 40-48 and 49-57) with a double imperative, " Cry aloud, spare not " (58: 1; cf. 40: 1; 49: 1).

2. He emphasizes true fasting and faithful Sabbath observance first (chapter 58). In verses 1-5, he rebukes the people because of the utter hollowness of their ritual; in verses 6-12, he counsels them to feed the hungry, house the poor and clothe the naked; while in verses 13-14, he promises them triumphant possession of their own land provided they cheerfully and faithfully sanctify the Sabbath (cf. 56: 2).

3. Originally there was but one legal fast day in the Hebrew calendar, the great Day of Atonement, on which it was enjoined to afflict not the body but the soul (Lev. 16: 29-31). The practice of fasting, however, was frequently resorted to by ancient Israel as a means of propitiating Deity (Judges 20: 26; 1 Sam. 7: 6; 12: 16, 21-23; 1 Kings 21: 12, 27), and as an expression of grief (1 Sam. 31: 13; 2 Sam. 1: 12). In Isaiah's day religion in general had degenerated into mere ceremonial (Isa. 1: 10-17). Men fasted and at the same time carried on their selfish secular employments (58: 3).

4. As with fasting, so with the observance of the Sabbath. All reverence for the seventh day had vanished. Accordingly, the prophet reminds Israel

that the Sabbath is holy ground which may not be trodden with irreverent feet: that it is a sanctuary, and " the holy of Jehovah "—a very remarkable designation for this most ancient of all sacred institutions (Gen. 2: 1-3)—and that Israel should delight in and honor it (58: 13-14).

Hindrances to Israel's Salvation Removed (Chapter 59)

1. It is Israel's sins, says the prophet, which have hidden Jehovah's face and retarded the nation's salvation. Their hands are defiled with blood; they speak lies and trust in vanity. " None sueth in righteousness." Murder, lying, injustice and violence fill the catalogue of their sins. The nation is wholly corrupt (59: 1-8). Such a picture is certainly too somber for the period of the exile, and it hardly describes the social conditions of Nehemiah's age; but it finds an almost exact counterpart in the prophecies of the eighth century B. C. (Isa. 1).

2. In verse 9 the prophet identifies himself with the people and leads them in their devotions. They confess that their sins testify against them (v. 12), and that they have denied Jehovah, practiced oppression, and spoken words of falsehood (v. 13). They therefore pray for peace and forgiveness, for light and justice (vs. 9-15).

3. With verse 15 the prophet's tone changes to that of anticipation. Jehovah is grieved over Israel's forlorn condition and, seeing their helplessness, he arms himself like a divine warrior to interfere judicially. He puts on righteousness as a coat of mail, sets upon his head the helmet of salvation, wears vengeance for clothing and zeal as a mantle, his only weapon being his arm, with which he brings salvation (vs. 15-19).

4. The scene is an ideal representation of the restoration of the nation from exile (cf. Rom. 11: 26). Israel shall be redeemed. With them as the nucleus of a new nation, Jehovah will enter anew into covenant relation, and put his Spirit upon them which shall abide with them henceforth and forever (vs. 20-21).

The Future Blessedness of Zion (Chapters 60-61)

1. Chapter 60 is the characteristic chapter of this section, containing a prophetic representation of the New Jerusalem. The long looked-for "light" (cf. 59: 9) begins to dawn: "Arise, shine; for thy light is come, and the glory of Jehovah is risen upon thee " (60: 1).

2. At this point the prophet paints a picture of the redeemed community. As in 2: 2-4 the Gentiles are seen flocking to Zion. They place their wealth at the disposal of the new Jewish state (60: 3-5). Israel's scattered sons also stream home by land and sea, like a " fleet of white sailed ships making for Palestinian havens and resembling a flock of doves speeding to their cotes " (60: 8-9).

3. Zion becomes the mistress of the nations. Foreigners build her walls, and her gates are kept open continually without fear of siege. The Gentiles acknowledge that Zion is the spiritual center of the world, whose walls denote "Salvation" and whose gates are called "Praise." Even Israel's oppressors regard Jerusalem as " the city of Jehovah, the Zion of the Holy One of Israel," and as " an eternal excellency," in which Jehovah sits as its everlasting light in the midst of a strong and victorious theocracy (60: 10-21).

4. In chapter 61, which Henry Drummond has called " the programme of Christianity," the Serv-

ant of Jehovah is again introduced, though anonymously, as the herald of salvation. " The Spirit of the Lord Jehovah is upon me; because Jehovah hath anointed me to preach good tidings unto the meek; he hath sent me to bind up the broken hearted, to proclaim liberty to the captives " (61: 1-3).

5. This gospel monologue of the Servant is followed by a promise of Jerusalem's restoration and blessedness (61: 4-11). Thus the prophecy moves steadily forward towards its goal in Jesus Christ (cf. Luke 4: 18-21).

Zion's Salvation Drawing Near
(Chapters 62:1 — 63:6)

1. Jehovah, who has long been silent (cf. 42: 14; 57: 11), resolves finally to bring his word to pass. " For Zion's sake will I not hold my peace, and for Jerusalem's sake I will not rest, until her righteousness go forth as brightness, and her salvation as a lamp that burneth" (62: 1).

2. Zion's salvation draweth near. Israel is urged to hasten their necessary preparation to depart out of captivity. " Go through, go through the gates; prepare ye the way of the people; cast up, cast up the highway; gather out the stones; lift up an ensign for the peoples. . . . Say ye to the daughter of Zion, Behold thy salvation cometh " (62: 10-11).

3. The nations will be spectators of the great event. A new name which will better symbolize her true character shall be given to Zion, namely, Hephzibah, "My delight is in her"; for Jerusalem shall no more be called Desolate. Judah too shall receive a new title which will better express the

new conditions, namely, Beulah, that is "Married";
for Jehovah delighteth in her, and her land shall
be married (62: 2-5; cf. 54: 5).

4. On the other hand, Zion's enemies will all be
vanquished. In a brief poem of peculiar dramatic
beauty (63: 1-6), the prophet portrays Jehovah's
vengeance as a victorious warrior, upon all those
who would retard Israel's deliverance. " Who is
this that cometh from Edom, with dyed garments
from Bozrah? . . . I have trodden the wine press
alone; and of the peoples there was no man with
me; yea, I trod them in mine anger, and trampled
them in my wrath; and their life-blood is sprinkled
upon my garments" (63: 1, 3).

5. Edom was Israel's inveterate foe. Hence the
prophet represents Jehovah's judgment of the nations as taking place on Edom's unhallowed soil.
Jehovah, whose mighty arm has wrought salvation,
returns as victor, having slain all of *Israel's* foes.
The poem is " a drama of divine vengeance."

Jehovah's "Servants" at Prayer
(Chapters 63:7 — 64:12)

1. Jehovah's "servants" (63: 17) resort to
prayer. The prophet undertakes to put into words
their feelings of thanksgiving, confession and sup-
plication (63: 7—64: 12). The prayer is one of
the most passionate utterances of its kind in the
Old Testament. It is both progressive and com-
prehensive.

2. First, Israel's past under Moses is reviewed
and Jehovah's lovingkindness to his chosen nation
is made the basis of an appeal for renewed mercy.
Forgiveness, they urge, is not founded on Israel's
trust in God, but rather on God's trust in them,

and his willingness to give them a fresh start
(63: 8-9).

3. They are fully conscious of having rebelled
and grieved his holy Spirit. Only here and in
Psalm 51: 11 in the Old Testament is the term
"holy Spirit" used as the personal designation of
God's ethical nature. " Jehovah" and "the angel
of his presence" and the "holy Spirit" are here distinguished "as three existences; an unmistakable
intimation of the mystery of the triune nature of
the one God, which is revealed in historical fulfilment in the New Testament work of redemption."
(Delitzsch.)

4. They also appeal to Jehovah as the Begetter
and Father of the nation (63: 16; 64: 8). With
this thought of the fatherhood of God, Isaiah had
opened his very first oracle to Judah and Jerusalem (1: 2). The idea of Jehovah's fatherhood is
rare in the Old Testament; still rarer the conception that Jehovah had caused Israel to err from his
ways (63: 17).

5. As the prayer proceeds the language becomes
increasingly impetuous. The people are thrown
into despair because Jehovah seems to have abandoned them altogether (63: 19). Accordingly they
cry out most passionately, "Oh, that thou wouldest
rend the heavens, that thou wouldest come down"
(64: 1)! They recognize that Jerusalem's condition is desperate. "Our holy and our beautiful
house, where our fathers praised thee, is burned
with fire: and all our pleasant places are laid
waste " (64: 11). Such language, however, is the
language of fervent prayer and must not be taken
with rigid literalness, as 63: 18 and 3: 8 plainly
show.

Jehovah's Answer, Zion Triumphant
(Chapters 65-66)

1. Jehovah answers his people's supplications,

distinguishing sharply between his own "servants" and Israel's apostates (chapters 65-66). Only his chosen "seed" shall be delivered (65: 9).

2. Those who have obdurately provoked Jehovah by sacrificing in gardens (65: 3; 66: 17), offering libations to Fortune and Destiny (65: 11), sitting among the graves to obtain oracles from the dead, and, like the Egyptians, eating swine's flesh and broth of abominable things which were supposed to possess magical properties, lodging in vaults or crypts in which heathen mysteries were celebrated (65: 4), and at the same time fancying that by celebrating such heathen mysteries they were holier than others and thereby disqualified to discharge the ordinary duties of life (65: 5)— such Jehovah designs to punish, measuring their work into their bosom and destroying them utterly with the sword (65: 7, 12).

3. On the other hand, the "servants" of Jehovah shall inherit his holy mountains. They shall rejoice and sing for joy of heart, and bless themselves in the God of Amen, i. e., in the God of Truth (65: 9, 14, 16). Jehovah will create new heavens and a new earth, men will live and grow old like the patriarchs, they will possess houses and vineyards and enjoy them; for an era of idyllic peace will be ushered in with the coming of the Messianic age, in which even the natures of wild animals will be changed and the most rapacious beasts will live together in harmony (65: 17-25).

4. Religion will become spiritual and decentralized, mystic cults will disappear, incredulous scoffers will be silenced, Zion's population will be marvelously multiplied, and the people will be comforted and rejoice (66: 1-14). Furthermore, all nations will flock to Zion to behold Jehovah's glory, and from one new moon to another, and from one Sabbath to another, all flesh will come up to worship in Jerusalem (66: 15-23).

5. But those who sacrifice to idols and practice occult and mystic rites will be punished with fire and whirlwind and sword, and their dead bodies lying about the city will be a visible spectacle of divine warning and an emphatic proof of God's punitive justice (66: 24). [This last verse of the book of Isaiah is the basis of the later Jewish conception of Gehenna, or hell, as the place of everlasting punishment.]

Concluding Observations

1. It is evident that the book of Isaiah closes practically as it begins, with a polemic against false worship, and the alternate reward of the righteous and punishment of the wicked. The prophet's audience from first to last consisted of two classes: (1) those who were formal and stereotyped in their religious observances (58: 3-6; cf. 1: 10-17), rebellious in heart (65: 2; cf. 1: 2, 23), ever provoking Jehovah to his face (65: 3; cf. 3: 8), guilty of violence and bloodshed (59: 6, 7; cf. 1: 15), sunken in idolatry and practicing foreign mysteries (65: 3-11; cf. 2: 6-8), sacrificing in gardens—a custom not mentioned in the Old Testament outside the book of Isaiah (65: 3; 66: 17; cf. 1: 29), who, because of their transgressions, are destined to be destroyed (66: 24; cf. 1: 24-31); and (2) the righteous, who are to be redeemed (65: 9; cf. 6: 13), and enjoy paradisaic peace, even the wild beasts sharing in and contributing to their joy and happiness (65: 25; cf. 11: 6-9).

2. The only essential difference between the prophet's earlier and later oracles is this: Isaiah in his riper years, on the basis of nearly half a century's experience, paints a much brighter eschatological picture than was possible in his early ministry. His picture of the Messianic age not only transcends those of his contemporaries in the

eighth century B. C., but he penetrates regions beyond the spiritual horizon of any and all other Old Testament seers. Such language as that contained in 66: 1-2 in particular, anticipates the great principle enunciated by Jesus in John 4: 24, namely, that " God is a Spirit: and they that worship him must worship in spirit and truth."

3. To attempt to date such oracles as these on the basis of internal evidence is an absolute impossibility. Ordinary prophecy may indeed within limits be dated in this way; not so these later oracles of Isaiah. They are not ordinary; they are extraordinary;   they   are   theology.   Humanly speaking one epoch could produce such revelations quite as easily as another.   But no epoch could have produced them apart from the Divine Spirit.

It Pleased Jehovah, for His Righteousness' Sake, to Magnify the Law, and Make It Honorable.

Isa. 42: 21.

For Thou art Our Father, though Abraham Knoweth Us not, and Israel Doth not Acknowledge Us: Thou, O Jehovah, art Our Father; Our Redeemer from Everlasting is Thy Name.

Isa. 63: 16.

For, Behold, I Create New Heavens and a New Earth; and the Former Things Shall not be Remembered, nor Come into Mind.

Isa. 65: 17.

As One Whom His Mother Comforteth, so will I Comfort You; and Ye Shall be Comforted in Jerusalem.

Isa. 66: 13.

And It Shall Come to Pass, That from one New Moon to another, and from one Sabbath to another, Shall all Flesh Come to Worship before Me, Saith Jehovah.

Isa. 66: 23.

STUDY FIFTEEN

REVIEW QUESTIONS

Studies One and Two

I.—ISAIAH'S LIFE AND WRITINGS

1. Recount the chief points in Isaiah's personal history.

2. Give an account of his call to the prophetic office.

3. Define his political and spiritual horizon.

4. In what sense was Isaiah a genuine patriot?

5. What is to be said of his literary genius and style?

6. What does tradition say concerning his end?

7. Mention some of the latest literature on Isaiah.

II.—ANALYSIS OF THE BOOK OF ISAIAH

1. Name the six general divisions of Isaiah's book.

2. Give a somewhat minute analysis of chapters 1-12.

3. Mention the foreign nations, whose fortunes affected Judah and Jerusalem, against whom Isaiah prophesied in chapters 13-23.

4. Summarize the contents of Jehovah's world-judgment in chapters 24-27.

5. Give the gist of Isaiah's warnings in chapters 28-33 against alliance with Egypt.

6. Show the relation of the historical section in chapters 36-39 both to that which precedes and that which follows.

7. Give a general analysis of chapters 40-66.

Studies Three and Four
III.—THE PERIOD OF ISAIAH

1. Describe the conditions which prevailed in western Asia, especially in Judah, under Uzziah.

2. What new world-power broke over the horizon during the reign of Jotham?

3. Give the details of the Syro-Ephraimitic war.

4. Trace the events which led up to the crisis of 722 B. C.

5. Tell something about Sargon II. and his relation to Merodach-Baladan.

6. Describe in chronological order the principal events of the year 701 B. C.

7. What was Judah's condition, socially, politically and religiously, during the closing years of Isaiah's ministry?

IV.—ISAIAH'S PROPHECIES CHRONOLOGICALLY ARRANGED

1. Of what value is the editorial arrangement of Isaiah's prophecies in attempting to date his oracles chronologically?

2. Which probably were Isaiah's earliest messages?

3. Which oracles are to be associated with the crisis of 734 B. C.?

4. Which prophecies seem to have sprung from the dark period just prior to the downfall of Samaria?

5. Name those prophecies which pretty certainly date from the period of Sargon's reign over Assyria.

6. Which sections of Isaiah's book seem to have had their origin shortly prior to the invasion of Sennacherib in 701 B. C.?

7. To what degree would oracles like those in chapters 40-66 bring comfort to the inhabitants of Judah and Jerusalem after the crisis of 701 B. C.?

Studies Five and Six

V.—THE CRITICAL PROBLEM

1. What portions of the book do critics allow to be genuine?

2. Criticise the fundamental axiom of modern criticism.

3. Mention certain governing criteria.

4. What should be one's attitude to the problem?

5. Sketch briefly the critical disintegration of the book.

6. Are chapters 40-66 considered a unity?

7. Trace the literary history of Isaiah's book.

VI.—JUDAH'S SOCIAL SINS (CHAPTERS 1-6)

1. What place does religion occupy in the well-being of society?

2. Describe Isaiah's attitude to war.

3. What was Judah's besetting sin?

4. To what extent were the upper classes responsible for the nation's moral condition?

5. Give a catalogue of Judah's national sins.

6. What was the condition of the masses?

7. What were the inevitable consequences of the nation's downward tendency?

Studies Seven and Eight

VII.—JUDAH'S POLITICAL ENTANGLEMENTS (CHAPTERS 7-12)

1. Describe the Syro-Ephraimitic uprising and its effect upon King Ahaz.

2. In what sense is the " Immanuel " passage, in 7: 14, Messianic?

3. Define "conspiracy" in its religious sense.

4. Why did Jehovah find it necessary to send judgment on North Israel?

5. What use did God make of Assyria in disciplining Judah?

6. Describe the prophet's vision of Israel's return from exile.

7. Correlate the distinctively Messianic passages (7: 14; 9: 6-7; 11: 1-2), and observe carefully their historical setting.

VIII.—"BURDENS" CONCERNING FOREIGN NATIONS (CHAPTERS 13-23)

1. What great lessons are taught by the oracles concerning Babylon?

2. Give the principal points of interest in the oracle against Moab.

3. What were Isaiah's messages to Philistia and Damascus, respectively?

4. In what way are Egypt and Ethiopia described as sharing in Jerusalem salvation?

5. Account for the prophet's almost sympathetic attitude toward Edom.

6. Who was Shebna? Why was he deposed from office?

7. Give a brief outline of the oracle against Tyre.

IX.—Spiritual Messages of Salvation (Chapters
24-27)

1. Distinguish between prophecy and apocalypse.

2. What is the significance, respectively, of the terms "earth" and "city" in these chapters?

3. Account for the optimistic tone of the various songs contained in these prophecies.

4. In what sense is life from the dead promised?

5. What was Jehovah's object in chastising his people?

6. What seems to have been the historic standpoint of the author of these chapters?

7. What was their practical value to Isaiah's own age?

X.—A Series of Six Woes (Chapters 28-33)

1. Give the gist of Isaiah's warning to the scoffing politicians of his time.

2. Account for the tone of his "woe" against Ariel.

3. What reproof does he give to those of Jerusalem who were hiding their plans from God?

4. Summarize the prophet's vehement arraignment of the pro-Egyptian party.

5. Describe the Messianic era which will eventually dawn upon Judah.

6. What is the substance of Isaiah's "woe" against Assyria?

7. Recount the promises corresponding to the prophet's several "woes."

Studies Eleven and Twelve

XI.—History, Prophecy and Song (Chapters 36-39)

1. Explain the phrase "the fourteenth year of King Hezekiah."

2. Describe Sennacherib's two attempts to take Jerusalem.

3. Give the contents of Isaiah's last formal prophecy concerning Assyria.

4. Tell the story of Hezekiah's sickness and recovery.

5. Sketch in outline Hezekiah's song of thanksgiving for extended life.

6. What was the significance of Merodach-Baladan's embassy?

7. Give an estimate of Hezekiah's character and work.

XII.—Deliverance from Captivity through Cyrus (Chapters 40-48)

1. Trace the argument of chapter 40 and its bearing upon Israel's condition.

2. What does the prophet argue is the supreme proof of Jehovah's sole deity?

3. Upon what two agents, temporal and spiritual, does Israel's future depend?

4. What pledge does Jehovah give of Israel's deliverance?

5. Mention some of the titles bestowed upon Cyrus, and show the historical relation of Cyrus to the prophet.

6. What great event will herald Israel's coming salvation?

7. Give a summary of the entire argument in chapters 40-48.

Studies Thirteen and Fourteen

XIII.—THE SERVANT OF JEHOVAH (CHAPTERS 49-57)

1. Name the four so-called distinctively " Servant Songs," and give some idea of their prophetic setting.

2. What are the Servant's functions in 42: 1-9?

3. Point out the new features concerning the Servant in 49: 1-13.

4. How is the Servant described in 50: 4-11?

5. Describe the Servant's character and sufferings as portrayed in 52: 13—53: 12.

6. Who probably is the Servant of Jehovah?

7. Show how these prophecies concerning the Servant have been fulfilled in Christ.

XIV.—THE FUTURE GLORY OF THE PEOPLE OF GOD (CHAPTERS 58-66)

1. What is taught concerning fasting and Sabbath observance?

2. Mention some of the hindrances to Israel's salvation which Jehovah promises to remove.

3. Describe the future blessedness of Zion as depicted in chapters 60-61.

4. What are the signs that Israel's salvation draweth near?

5. Give an analysis of Israel's passionate prayer for deliverance.

6. What is Jehovah's gracious response?

7. Show how the book of Isaiah begins and ends with essentially the same general thoughts.

FAMILIAR PHRASES FROM ISAIAH

The whole head is sick and the whole heart faint (1: 5).

Wise in their own eyes (5: 21).

Woe is me (6: 5).

Here am I, send me (6: 8).

A little child shall lead them (11: 6).

The earth shall be full of the knowledge of the Lord, as the waters cover the sea (11: 9).

Blessed be Egypt (19: 25).

Watchman, what of the night (21: 11)?

Let us eat and drink; for to-morrow we die (22: 13).

A feast of fat things (25: 6).

God will wipe away tears from off all faces (25: 8).

Precept upon precept, line upon line (28: 10).

A covenant with death (28: 15).

A precious corner stone (28: 16).

Draw near to me with their lips but their heart is far from me (29: 13).

Speak unto us smooth things (30: 10).

Bread of adversity and water of affliction (30: 20).

This is the way, walk ye in it (30: 21).

Ye shall have a song as in the night (30: 29).

As the shadow of a great rock in a weary land (32: 2).

The heavens shall be rolled together as a scroll (34: 4).

The desert shall rejoice and blossom as the rose (35: 1).

The lame man shall leap as an hart (35: 6).

The wayfaring man though a fool shall not err therein (35: 8).

Set thine house in order: for thou shalt die and not live (38: 1).

All flesh is grass (40: 6).

As a drop of a bucket (40: 15).

He feedeth on ashes (44: 20).

World without end (45: 17).

Unto me every knee shall bow (45: 23).

Even to old age and hoar hairs (46: 4).

In the furnace of affliction (48: 10).

Lick the dust (49: 23).

I set my face like a flint (50: 7).

Wax old as a garment (50: 9).

The rock whence ye are hewn and the hole whence ye are digged (51: 1).

See eye to eye (52: 8).

As a root out of a dry ground, having no form or comeliness (53: 2).

A man of sorrows (53: 3).

All we like sheep have gone astray (53: 6).

Brought as a lamb to the slaughter (53: 7).

Lengthen thy cords and strengthen thy stakes (54: 2).

The mountains shall depart and the hills be removed (54: 10).

No weapon that is formed against thee shall prosper (54: 17).

Without money and without price (55: 1).

For my thoughts are not your thoughts (55: 8).

Like the troubled sea (57: 20).

Make thy officers peace, and thine exactors righteousness (60: 17).

The oil of joy for mourning and the garment of praise for the spirit of heaviness (61: 3).

The garments of salvation (61: 10).

Beulah land (62: 4).

As the bridegroom rejoiceth over the bride (62: 5).

Mighty to save (63: 1).
Trodden the winepress alone (63: 3).
The angel of his presence (63: 9).
Rend the heavens and come down (64: 1).

We all do fade as a leaf (64: 6).
I am holier than thou (65: 5).
The God of truth (65: 16).
Shall not labor in vain (65: 23).
A nation shall be born in a day (66: 8).
Peace like a river (66: 12; 48: 18).
Their worm shall not die, neither shall their fire be quenched (66: 24).

INDEX

Roman Numerals refer to Studies; Italics to authors cited.

THE BOOK OF ISAIAH